URBAN TRAILS
TRAILS

SACRAMENTO

URBAN
TRAILS
SACRAMENTO

**Davis · Elk Grove
Folsom · Sierra Foothills**

JOHN SOARES

MOUNTAINEERS
BOOKS

For my favorite Sacramento people: Micaila, Zoey,
Paisley, and Lucinda Walton, and Michelle Alexander

 MOUNTAINEERS BOOKS is dedicated
to the exploration, preservation, and enjoyment
of outdoor and wilderness areas.

1001 SW Klickitat Way, Suite 201, Seattle, WA 98134
800-553-4453, www.mountaineersbooks.org

Printed in China
Distributed in the United Kingdom by Cordee, www.cordee.co.uk

First edition, 2021

Copyeditor: Ginger Oppenheimer
Design: Jen Grable
Layout: Jennifer Shontz, www.redshoedesign.com
Cartographer: Pease Press
All photographs by the author unless credited otherwise
Cover photograph: *Foresthill Divide Loop Trail (Trail 18) in Auburn State
Recreation Area*
Frontispiece: *Dry Creek Greenway (Trail 5) in Roseville*

Library of Congress Cataloging-in-Publication Data is on file for this title
at https://lccn.loc.gov/2020022456. The ebook record is available at
https://lccn.loc.gov/2020022457.

Mountaineers Books titles may be purchased for corporate, educational, or
other promotional sales, and our authors are available for a wide range of
events. For information on special discounts or booking an author, contact
our customer service at 800-553-4453 or mbooks@mountaineersbooks.org.

Printed on FSC®-certified materials

ISBN (paperback): 978-1-68051-284-7
ISBN (ebook): 978-1-68051-285-4

An independent nonprofit publisher since 1960

CONTENTS

DOWNTOWN SACRAMENTO

GREATER SACRAMENTO URBAN AREA

SIERRA FOOTHILLS

SOUTH OF SACRAMENTO

WEST OF SACRAMENTO

TRAIL LOCATOR

TRAILS AT A GLANCE

Trail and/or Park	Distance	Walk	Hike	Run	Kids	Dogs
DOWNTOWN SACRAMENTO						
1. Discovery Park	4.4 miles roundtrip	•		•	•	•
2. Capitol Park and Old Sacramento	3.5 miles of paths	•			•	•
3. William Land Park	3.0 miles of trails	•		•	•	•
GREATER SACRAMENTO URBAN AREA						
4. Gibson Ranch Regional Park	2.6-mile loop	•		•	•	•
5. Dry Creek Greenway	2.8 miles roundtrip	•		•	•	•
6. Mather Regional Park	1.6 miles roundtrip	•			•	•
7. William B. Pond Recreation Area	Up to 2.0 miles of trails	•		•	•	•
8. Effie Yeaw Nature Center Loop	1.3-mile loop	•	•		•	
9. Sacramento Bar	Up to 8.0 miles of trails	•	•	•	•	•
10. Lake Natoma Loop	10.9-mile loop	•		•	•	•
11. Mormon Island Cove to Browns Ravine	4.8 miles roundtrip		•	•	•	•
12. Dotons Cove Trail	1.0 mile roundtrip	•	•		•	•
SIERRA FOOTHILLS						
13. Hidden Falls Regional Park	4.2 miles roundtrip		•	•		•
14. Stevens Trail	7.0 miles roundtrip		•	•		•
15. Mountain Quarries Railroad Trail	3.4 miles roundtrip	•		•	•	•
16. Pointed Rocks	4.6 miles roundtrip		•	•		•

Trail and/or Park	Distance	Walk	Hike	Run	Kids	Dogs
17. Lake Clementine Trail	4.6 miles roundtrip		•	•	•	•
18. Foresthill Divide Loop Trail	9.2-mile loop		•	•		•
19. Cronan Ranch Regional Trails Park	4.1-mile loop		•	•		•
20. Dave Moore Nature Area	1.2-mile loop	•	•		•	•
21. Marshall Gold Discovery State Historic Park	3.3-mile loop	•	•	•	•	•
SOUTH OF SACRAMENTO						
22. Blue Heron Trails	0.7 mile of trails	•			•	
23. River Walk Trail	3.8 miles roundtrip	•			•	
24. Wetlands Walk and Boardwalk Trails	1.6 miles roundtrip	•			•	
25. Lodi Lake Nature Trail	1.3-mile loop	•		•	•	
26. Howard Ranch Trail	7.1 miles roundtrip	•		•	•	
WEST OF SACRAMENTO						
27. Cache Creek Nature Preserve	2.0 miles of trails	•		•	•	•
28. Yolo Bypass Wildlife Area: Pond Walk	1.8 miles roundtrip	•			•	
29. Yolo Bypass Wildlife Area Loop	2.3-mile loop	•			•	
30. Covell Greenbelt	2.4-mile loop	•		•	•	•
31. UC Davis Arboretum	3.5-mile loop	•		•	•	•
32. Putah Creek Riparian Reserve	2.7 miles of trails	•		•	•	•
33. Putah Creek Nature Park	2.0 miles roundtrip	•		•	•	•
34. Blue Ridge Trail	5.4 miles roundtrip		•			
35. Homestead Trail	2.4 miles roundtrip		•		•	

INTRODUCTION
TRAILS FOR FUN AND FITNESS IN YOUR BIG BACKYARD

UNTIL ABOUT A HUNDRED YEARS ago, most people lived in rural areas and the natural world was an integral part of daily life. Now many of us live in cities or in suburbs adjacent to cities. And too often we let the bustle and distraction of daily life—work, traffic, family and social commitments, phones, computers, the internet, television—keep us from paying much attention to nature, let alone spending significant time in it. There's good news, though. For decades, states, counties, cities, and towns across the country have been acquiring land and creating parks and recreation areas with trail systems, and the Sacramento area is no exception.

Urban Trails: Sacramento covers a wide variety of trails for all abilities and ages in Sacramento itself and in the surrounding towns, hills, and valleys, allowing you to experience nature in your life on a daily or weekly basis. Whether you are a hardcore hiker, someone who likes flat and easy walks, a parent with young children, or a runner looking for new trails, *Urban Trails: Sacramento* provides detailed information so you can easily identify and then enjoy the perfect hike, trail, or path near you.

Downtown Sacramento—Old Sacramento and the capitol region near the intersection of I-5 and Business 80—serves as the central hub of the book with the first three hikes. The book

Coon Creek in Hidden Falls Regional Park (Trail 13)

then moves east along I-80 and US Highway 50 to cover trail systems in Roseville, Folsom, and other towns, including several along the American River and around Folsom Lake. The next region includes Auburn State Recreation Area and nearby areas in the Sierra Nevada foothills. Then come hikes in the Central Valley south of Sacramento, including trails in the Cosumnes River Preserve. The book then heads west to cover several hikes in and near Davis before ending in the Coast Range foothills near Lake Berryessa.

This guidebook has two main objectives. The first is to help you boost your physical fitness. Whether you're walking, running, or biking, book in hand, you can get on a nearby trail just about every day of the year.

The second objective is to help you boost your mental health. Studies show that spending time in nature improves cognitive abilities and increases happiness. Plus, when you hike with friends or family, you build social relationships, which also benefit mental health.

Sacramento and its surrounding areas continue to grow, but so do opportunities to walk, hike, and bike. Whether you live here or visit here, use this book to get outside and get more out of life.

HOW TO USE
THIS GUIDE

THIS BOOK IS ORGANIZED TO make it easy to choose the best trails for you and your hiking companions. I've walked every step of these paths, so you can be confident that all the information is accurate at the time of publication. However, regulations can change and trails can temporarily close, so always check with the managing agency for current conditions. You can find agency contact info in the Resources section in the back of the book.

THE DESTINATIONS

This book covers thirty-five trails and trail systems in and around Greater Sacramento, including downtown, the suburbs, the Sacramento Valley, and the nearby Sierra Nevada foothills, including Auburn State Recreation Area.

Each route description begins with the trail name or park name, followed by a block of information that details the following:

Distance. Here you will find roundtrip mileage or a total mileage of trails.

Elevation gain. The total amount of elevation you'll climb over the course of the route is given in feet. This number

Late afternoon in Davis's Covell Greenbelt (Trail 30)

takes into account all the ups and downs, not just the difference between the starting point and the high point.

High point. The highest point of elevation you reach during the journey is also provided in feet.

Difficulty. The five categories of difficulty are easy, easy to moderate, moderate, moderate to challenging, and challenging. A subjective measurement, the difficulty level is an estimate of the total effort required to complete the route. It primarily reflects total distance and elevation gain but can also take into account short, steep stretches of rough, difficult-to-negotiate trail. Always assess the abilities of the least able person in your group when picking a hike.

Fitness. This category indicates whether the trail is best suited to walkers, hikers, or runners. Paved paths that are mostly level will appeal to walkers and runners and to people with mobility issues or with small children and perhaps a baby stroller. Trails designated for hikers have narrower, unpaved paths that typically have more elevation gain. Of course, a

Lupine and lichen in the Sierra foothills

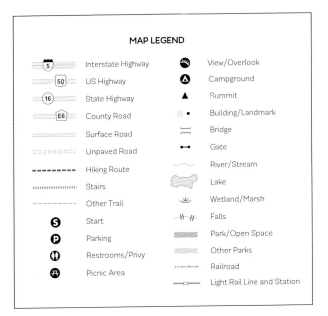

MAP LEGEND

Interstate Highway	View/Overlook
US Highway	Campground
State Highway	Summit
County Road	Building/Landmark
Surface Road	Bridge
Unpaved Road	Gate
Hiking Route	River/Stream
Stairs	Lake
Other Trail	Wetland/Marsh
Start	Falls
Parking	Park/Open Space
Restrooms/Privy	Other Parks
Picnic Area	Railroad
	Light Rail Line and Station

dedicated hiker can walk a level, paved path, and a hard-core runner can run on steep dirt trails.

Family-friendly. This field indicates the suitability of a route for children twelve years old and younger. It may also mention fun attractions for kids, any specific hazards such as cliffs, and multiuse trails where bike use is common.

Dog-friendly. This description lets you know if your pooch is welcome and under what rules (on-leash only, under strict voice command, etc.). Always have a leash with you.

Bike-friendly. Here you will find whether bikes are allowed, regulations on bike use, and any information relevant to biking on trails and paths.

Amenities. Park, recreation area, and other trail amenities can include features such as restrooms, picnic tables, drinking fountains, playgrounds, interpretive nature panels, and campgrounds, among others.

Contact/map. In this field, you will find the name of the route's managing agency, which is the main contact for current trail conditions and further information that could affect your access to and enjoyment of the trails. Most agencies offer a downloadable map (often high quality); if no map is available online, it will be indicated here. See Trail and Park Management Agencies in the Resources section for website addresses and phone numbers.

GPS. The GPS coordinates for the main trailhead appear here in degrees and decimal minutes (based on WGS84 datum).

More key info. Here you'll find information about whether a trail or park charges a fee or requires a permit, as well as hours of operation, seasonal closures, and anything else relevant to your ability to access and enjoy the trails.

GETTING THERE. Driving: This section provides directions to the trailhead from the nearest town, freeway exit, or major road intersection and gives details on parking. (Note: There are often multiple ways to access trailheads, especially in Sacramento and the greater urban area, depending on where you are driving from.) **Transit:** If public transportation serves the trailhead, you'll find the agency and line number here as well as the bus stop closest to the trailhead.

HIKE OVERVIEW. The overview describes key features of the trail or park, including notable geographic details and history. This brief description can help you choose the best outing for you and your companions.

GET MOVING. This section, the longest of each destination, provides specific guidance on where to go on the trails and how to get there along with descriptions of what you might experience along the way.

GO FARTHER. Finally I offer suggestions, where applicable, for extending your hike, walk, or run on other paths within the park system or nearby.

PERMITS, REGULATIONS, AND PARK FEES

Some of the trails and parks in this book require an entrance fee, primarily those in the Sacramento Regional Park system, Folsom Lake State Recreation Area, Auburn State Recreation Area, and Marshall Gold Discovery State Historic Park. Both the Sacramento Regional Park system and state parks sell annual passes that can save you a lot of money if you visit the parks more than a few times each year.

The information block at the beginning of each route description provides details of regulations governing dogs and trail use, restricted hours and dates, and whether or not an entrance fee or pass is required. Regulations can change; it's always a good idea to check the managing agency's website and call the main phone number if you have questions about current conditions and requirements.

ROAD AND TRAIL CONDITIONS

Trail conditions rarely change drastically from year to year. That said, the usability and accessibility of trails (and access roads to more remote trails) can change, especially after major weather events or during road construction work. Heavy rains can wash out sections of trail, and strong winds can blow large trees across trails. The same can happen to access roads, especially dirt roads. That's why it's always a good idea to check with the managing agency before heading out, particularly for the more remote trails like those in the foothills east of Sacramento.

Volunteer organizations play a big role in maintaining trails throughout the country, including in the Sacramento area. Consider joining one or more of these organizations and helping out on trail-maintenance days. See Trail and Conservation Organizations in the Resources section at the back of the book.

OUTDOOR ETHICS

Outdoor ethics means taking personal responsibility for minimizing your impact on the natural environment and leaving it as undisturbed as possible for others to enjoy, whether you frequent a remote trail or an urban path.

Pack it in, pack it out. Always take your own garbage with you when you leave and dispose of it properly or recycle or reuse it when possible. Extra points for packing out trash that others have left behind.

Safely dispose of human waste. Most parks have restrooms at the trailhead. If you have to relieve yourself out on the trail, stay well away (ideally 200 feet or more) from water sources, camps, and trails when you urinate; travel a minimum of 200 feet away from water and far from trails and campsites to defecate. If you need to defecate, dig a hole six to ten inches deep, preferably in forest duff, where the feces will decompose relatively rapidly. Bring a sealable plastic bag to pack out used toilet paper.

TRAIL ETIQUETTE

Enhance your wilderness experience and those of other park users by practicing basic rules of trail etiquette. The one underlying rule: be courteous and always use common sense.

Observe the right of way. In some parks hikers share the path with cyclists and equestrians. Hikers are more mobile and should move off the trail to let cyclists and equestrians pass.

Move aside for horses. When you meet people on horseback, step off the trail to the downhill side whenever possible. If you must go to the uphill side, crouch down so you do not tower above the horses. Speak to the riders in a calm and normal voice. If you brought your dog, keep it under firm control at your side.

Stay on the trail. Do not shortcut trail switchbacks or create new trails, both of which cause erosion and can require expensive and time-consuming repairs.

Young mallards in William Land Park (Trail 3)

Follow the rules. Each park has specific rules for what is and isn't allowed. Make sure you read the rules, which are usually posted prominently at trailheads and often at various points in the park. Typical rules govern which types of users can use which trails.

Keep your dog under control. Many of us love to bring the pooch when we hike. Make sure dogs are allowed and that you follow all rules, including leash rules. Even if dogs are allowed off-leash, you should always have a leash with you in case you need to keep your dog at your side or away from other dogs, animals, or people. Be considerate of others who may not want to interact with your dog. Finally, bring poop bags to collect your dog's droppings and make sure you dispose of them properly.

Avoid disturbing wildlife. Observe animals and birds from a distance. This not only increases your safety, it also allows critters to engage in normal behavior and not have to react to your presence.

Take only photographs. Leave all natural and human features exactly as you found them.

Mind the noise. Neither the critters nor your fellow hikers want to hear your music, your shouts, or your loud voice. Keep your noise production way down and speak at a normal conversational volume.

Many of these guidelines were established by the Leave No Trace Center for Outdoor Ethics. Visit https://lnt.org to learn more about best practices in the outdoors to minimize your effect on the environment and other trail users.

POTENTIAL HAZARDS

Exploring trails is overall quite safe. However, you do need to pay attention to animals, insects, and plants that can potentially be hazardous. There is also the danger of wildfire, pertinent here for Trails 34–35, both which are closed on Cal Fire red flag days. Learn more at www.fire.ca.gov.

BEARS

Of the trails described in this book, you are most likely to see a bear (or a mountain lion or a rattlesnake) in the Sierra Nevada foothills east of Sacramento. Most black bears will zoom away at warp speed when they spot you. You can, however, definitely upset a bear if you surprise it on the trail; a mother bear in particular can feel threatened if you pass between her and her cubs. If you encounter a bear, speak in a calm voice about your peaceful intentions as you slowly back away; do not turn and run. In the highly unlikely event that an attack occurs, fight back and focus on the muzzle area. Although the grizzly bear is featured on the state flag, the species has been eradicated from California.

MOUNTAIN LIONS

Most hikers go their entire lives without spotting even one of these large predators, and for good reason: mountain lions require a lot of territory, and they usually avoid humans. If a lion does approach you, pick up small children and leash your dogs. Hold your ground, extend your arms to look as large as possible, throw rocks, and shout. Do not run, crouch, or turn your back on the lion. If you're attacked, fight back.

RATTLESNAKES

Identified primarily by a jointed tail that rattles, rattlesnakes can inflict a potentially fatal bite, though they'll bite only if cornered or touched. Active in the warmer months in and around summer, they live under brush and in dry, rocky areas. To prevent bites, always look where you're going and be particularly careful about where you place your hands and feet when hiking cross-country. If a rattlesnake bites you, stay calm and relaxed and get to a hospital as soon as possible.

A NOTE ABOUT SAFETY

Safety is an important concern in all outdoor activities. No guidebook can alert you to every hazard or anticipate the limitations of every reader. Therefore, the descriptions of roads, trails, routes, and natural features in this book are not representations that a particular place or excursion will be safe for your party. When you follow any of the routes described in this book, you assume responsibility for your own safety. Under normal conditions, such excursions require the usual attention to traffic, road and trail conditions, weather, terrain, the capabilities of your party, and other factors. Because many of the lands in this book are subject to development or change of ownership, conditions may have changed since this book was written that make your use of some of these routes unwise. Always check for current conditions, obey posted private property signs, and avoid confrontations with property owners or managers. Keeping informed on current conditions and exercising common sense are the keys to a safe, enjoyable outing.

—*Mountaineers Books*

Friends enjoy the Lake Clementine Trail (Trail 17).

TICKS

These critters typically live in brushy and grassy areas, where they hope to catch a ride with an animal (such as you) so they can bore in and drink some fresh blood. The problem: some carry Lyme disease, which can make humans very ill. You can drastically lower the odds of a tick attaching to you by wearing a long-sleeve shirt along with long pants that you've tucked inside your socks. If a tick does attach, you can try to dislodge it with a tick removal kit, or you can head for the nearest doctor. If you remove a tick, freeze it in a plastic bag in case your doctor wants to test it for Lyme disease later. If you feel or see any unusual symptoms after a tick bite, such as a rash or joint stiffness or swelling, visit a doctor.

POISON OAK

Poison oak assumes a variety of confusing disguises ranging from small shrub to snaky vine. Part of the subterfuge is leaf shape, which varies from plant to plant. The telltale sign of poison oak (or for what could be poison oak) is a cluster of three leaves. Many people develop an itchy, red rash after contact with poison oak. If you think you touched poison oak, or touched someone or something that touched poison oak (a dog, for example), wash immediately with soap and cool water. The urushiol oil from the plant can linger on clothes, gear, and pets' fur until it is washed off. Many stores sell products that help suppress the symptoms.

WATER AND GEAR

For most routes in this book, you won't need to bring a lot of supplies. But no matter which route you choose, it's always a good idea to bring a small day pack with plenty of water, some healthy food, an extra layer of clothing, sun protection, and protection against rain if precipitation is in the forecast.

For longer hikes in wilder areas, use the Ten Essentials, developed by The Mountaineers, to make intelligent choices about what to pack.

THE TEN ESSENTIALS

1. **Navigation.** Carry a good map of the area encompassing your route and know how to read it. Typically, maps can be downloaded from the park website, or they may be available at the trailhead. Your cell phone can also be useful for navigation, but don't rely solely upon it.

2. **Headlamp.** If you unexpectedly find yourself still on the trail after dark, you'll be very glad to be able to see where you are going because you have a headlamp. Bring spare batteries. Most cell phones can also provide illumination (see if you need to download an app before you go), but using that function can quickly drain the battery.

3. **Sun protection.** Bring and use good sunscreen (rated at least SPF 30), along with a broad-brimmed hat, sunglasses, and sun-protective clothing. Bring all of these even on cloudy days; you never know when the sun will pop out.

4. **First aid.** Take a basic first-aid kit with bandages, blister prevention supplies, antiseptic, pain relievers, and tweezers. It's a good idea to bring antihistamine tablets in case of an allergic reaction. Also bring essential prescription medications.

5. **Knife.** A small pocketknife can be useful for a variety of purposes.

6. **Fire.** It's highly unlikely you'll need to spend an unplanned night on the trails described in this book; however, if you have to and you truly need the warmth of a fire, you'll be glad you are prepared. Bring a butane lighter or waterproof matches in a sealable bag; also bring something that easily burns, such as cotton balls, dryer lint, or a commercial firestarter.

7. **Shelter.** Even if you are not planning to be out overnight, bring something as basic as a large garbage bag or a rain poncho. Inexpensive and lightweight tarps and bivy sacks are also good options.

8. **Extra food.** Bring a substantial supply of nuts, trail mix, dried fruit, energy bars, and other healthy snacks.

9. **Extra water.** Bring more than enough water to keep you fully hydrated for the entire length of your hike, plus some extra. Include water purification tablets or a water filter in case you stay out longer than planned.

10. **Extra clothes.** Weather can change quickly. Be prepared for substantial drops in temperature by bringing extra layers and raingear. Make sure you have enough clothing to survive overnight, if necessary.

SAFETY CONCERNS

Trails and parks are generally quite safe. However, you should practice basic precautions such as always being aware of your surroundings and letting someone know where and when you are walking, hiking, or running, especially if you go alone.

Trailhead theft. Lower the probability that this rare event will happen to you by locking all car doors, tightly closing all car windows, and taking all valuables with you.

Potential threats from humans. Vagrancy and drug use occur in some urban parks. Stick to the trails and you are unlikely to encounter a homeless encampment. If you do come upon one, watch for human waste, needles, and other hazardous materials.

Despite these warnings, most areas are quite safe. Because these trails are often in urban areas, you should of course always exercise common sense and trust your judgment about a particular park or trail based on the current conditions.

Next page: *Leafy shade in William Land Park (Trail 3)*

DOWNTOWN SACRAMENTO

Sacramento, the capital of the most populous and economically powerful state in the United States, is also one of the fastest growing cities in California. Founded in 1848 near the confluence of the Sacramento and American Rivers to house and provide provisions and services for the thousands of miners searching for gold in the nearby Sierra Nevada foothills, the city grew quickly, becoming state capital in 1854.

Surviving the end of the gold rush and serious floods, Sacramento prospered in the late nineteenth century as the economic hub of the Central Valley. In the twentieth century, Sacramento also became the crossroads for Interstates 5 and 80, the two main freeways linking California to the rest of the West Coast and the United States.

Despite the burgeoning population and the needs of expanding business, the city preserved some land for recreation. This section focuses on three hikes in and near the downtown area. The first visits more tranquil areas along the north bank of the American River on the Jedediah Smith Memorial Trail. The second takes you into the heart of downtown by visiting Capitol Park and Old Sacramento, where you tour the capitol building and wander past historically significant nineteenth-century buildings near the Sacramento River. The third explores urban William Land Park, home of the Sacramento Zoo.

1   Discovery Park

DISTANCE:	4.4 miles roundtrip
ELEVATION GAIN:	Negligible
HIGH POINT:	30 feet
DIFFICULTY:	Easy
FITNESS:	Walkers, runners
FAMILY-FRIENDLY:	Yes
DOG-FRIENDLY:	On-leash
BIKE-FRIENDLY:	Yes
AMENITIES:	Bathrooms, picnic tables, water
CONTACT/MAP:	Sacramento County Regional Parks; download map from website
GPS:	N 38˚36.021', W 121˚30.460'
MORE KEY INFO:	Open sunrise to sunset daily; fee; wheelchair accessible; numerous cyclists

GETTING THERE

Driving: On I-5 just north of downtown Sacramento, take exit 521, signed for Garden Highway. Whether you are coming from the north or south on I-5, turn left on Garden Highway. Drive east on Garden Highway about 0.4 mile and watch closely for Natomas Park Drive and Discovery Park on the right, where you turn. Pay your fee at the entrance station then continue on the main paved road 0.4 mile to a stop sign. Go straight and then curve left for the final 0.1 mile to the large parking lot. Park near the two-lane bridge on the northeast side.

Transit: Bus 86 stops on Natomas Park Drive near Garden Highway. Cross Garden Highway, enter Discovery Park, and then either follow the driving directions above or walk straight toward the American River to find the trail.

This flat and easy hike in Discovery Park begins at the confluence of the American and Sacramento Rivers and follows

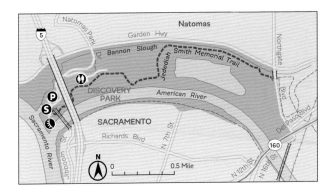

the American River upstream via the paved Jedediah Smith Memorial Trail to the turnaround point at Northgate Boulevard. Along the way you'll enjoy both water views and lush riparian vegetation.

GET MOVING

Before starting the official hike on the Jedediah Smith Memorial Trail, head to the right across the grass to the bank of the American River. Let your eyes follow the American River downstream to its meeting with the mighty Sacramento River. The American River originates high in the northern Sierra Nevada to the east, whereas the Sacramento River begins far to the north in the mountains just west of Mount Shasta. After taking in the waters of the American River, the Sacramento flows south and west to meet the San Joaquin River at the Sacramento–San Joaquin Delta, which then empties into the Pacific Ocean at San Francisco Bay.

Look for yellow concrete posts on the northeast side of the parking lot that indicate the beginning of the trail. You're in Discovery Park at the western end of the paved Jedediah Smith Memorial Trail (American River Bike Trail). The Jedediah Smith Memorial Trail (see "The America River Parkway"

Cottonwood trees shade the Jedediah Smith Memorial Trail in Discovery Park.

THE AMERICAN RIVER PARKWAY

The American River Parkway definitely deserves its appellation as the jewel of the Sacramento area. Stretching 29 miles along the American River from the confluence of the American River and the Sacramento River at Discovery Park all the way to Folsom Dam, the parkway allows residents and visitors the opportunity to escape the noise and bustle of city and suburban life to walk, cycle, picnic, and simply enjoy the natural beauty of the river and its riparian borders.

Efforts to create the American River Parkway initially began in the early 1960s. With the cooperation of federal, state, and local governments and agencies, plus the help of organizations like the American River Parkway Foundation and the support of local voters, the parkway has grown to include seventeen different parks. This book features trails in five of those parks, but there are numerous other places you can access the American River Parkway.

The paved multiuse Jedediah Smith Memorial Trail (also known as the American River Bike Trail) winds 32 miles through the American River Parkway from Discovery Park north of downtown Sacramento all the way to Beal's Point at Folsom Lake. Completed in 1985, the trail is named for the explorer Jedediah Smith (1799–1831) who led the first known expeditions of Americans to California and also traveled up the American River in 1827. The trail is very popular with walkers and cyclists and connects to many other paths, both paved and dirt.

sidebar) extends 32 miles along the American River through Sacramento County to end at Beal's Point on the west side of Folsom Lake.

The American River Parkway, which contains the Jedediah Smith Memorial Trail, is a favorite recreation destination for the region's walkers, runners, cyclists, and equestrians. Speaking of cyclists, they are quite frequent on the Jedediah Smith Memorial Trail; regulations require you to walk or run on the dirt on the left side of the pavement whenever feasible, which allows you to see oncoming cyclists and stay out of their way.

Walk east and quickly pass under a two-lane bicycle bridge and the route that leads to Old Sacramento and downtown. Stately California sycamore trees grow in abundance here, taking advantage of the deep, well-watered soil near the American River. You'll also note large valley oak and cottonwood trees, which also require rich soils with plenty of moisture. Reach a large sign that explains local natural history and then pass under I-5. Initially the roar of traffic is quite loud, but it fades gradually as you continue east.

Enjoy a view of the American River to the right at 0.2 mile as you wander through the developed portion of Discovery Park; numerous picnic tables are scattered in the shade to the left, and you'll see lush riparian vegetation to the right. Encounter black walnut trees and extensive blackberry patches and don't miss the California grapevines that climb up to forty feet into the trees.

At 0.3 mile, you'll find restrooms on the left. Wander under majestic valley oaks and in the spring pass a wildflower display that includes mustard and California poppy. Leave the developed portion of Discovery Park behind at 0.6 mile as the noise from I-5 fades. Thick vegetation borders both sides of the path while numerous cottonwood trees provide shade.

At 1.0 mile the Jedediah Smith Memorial Trail swings north and away from the American River. At 1.3 miles it turns east and crosses a paved road. You now pass between Bannon Slough on the left, which is lined with riparian vegetation, and a large wetland on the right that shrinks considerably over the course of summer but is always an excellent place for bird-watching.

Continue east between Bannon Slough and the wetland, with powerlines overhead and a bit of traffic noise from Garden Highway to the north, as you enjoy the intermittent shade of cottonwoods and valley oaks. At 2.2 miles reach a trail junction just before Northgate Boulevard, your turnaround point. From here, return to the trailhead the way you came.

2

Capitol Park and Old Sacramento

DISTANCE:	3.5 miles of paths
ELEVATION GAIN:	Negligible
HIGH POINT:	20 feet
DIFFICULTY:	Easy
FITNESS:	Walkers
FAMILY-FRIENDLY:	Yes
DOG-FRIENDLY:	On-leash
BIKE-FRIENDLY:	No
AMENITIES:	Bathrooms and water in capitol building, in Capitol Park, and in numerous businesses
CONTACT/MAP:	California State Capitol Museum; download map from website
GPS:	N 38°34.640', W 121°29.769'
MORE KEY INFO:	Always open; much of the suggested route is wheelchair accessible

GETTING THERE

Driving: Take the J Street exit off I-5 (exit 519B). Head east for several blocks through downtown Sacramento. Both street parking and multiple parking garages are available in the area (fee). The walk begins at Ninth Street at the east end of Capitol Mall, which is between L Street and N Street. L Street is two blocks to the right of J Street as you go east (and move up the numbered streets).

Transit: All three light rail lines and numerous buses serve downtown Sacramento, including Capitol Park and Old Sacramento.

This walk hits the historical highlights of downtown Sacramento. The route begins with the California State Capitol and its beautifully landscaped park and then travels Capitol Mall to Old Sacramento, home to the Sacramento River,

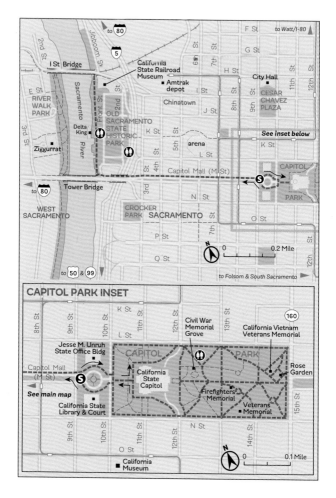

CAPITOL PARK INSET

Old Sacramento State Historic Park, and a wide variety of restaurants and other businesses. If you prefer, instead of the suggested route, you can park or get off public transportation wherever you like in the vicinity and design your own route.

The Rose Garden adds beautiful color to Capitol Park.

GET MOVING

Start on Ninth Street, where Capitol Mall stretches to the west and you'll see the California State Capitol directly ahead to the east. Walk east near the circular driveway between two imposing neoclassical buildings, the California State Library and Court on the right and the Jesse M. Unruh State Office Building on the left. (On your return to head west on Capitol Mall you'll again pass between these buildings.)

At Tenth Street the California State Capitol stretches in full glory before you. Built between 1860 and 1874, the massive neoclassical structure houses the state assembly, the state senate, the governor's office, and the California State Capitol Museum. The latter is well worth a visit as is the capitol building itself. Both are open every day except Thanksgiving, Christmas, and New Year's Day; check the California State Capitol Museum website for specific hours for both (see Resources).

Walk past a row of large deodar cedars on the north side of the capitol building to begin exploring the grounds of Capitol Park. A network of paved paths interweaves the entire area between the capitol and Fifteenth Street, allowing access to mature trees, both native and nonnative, plus other botanical features and various monuments.

Travel east past coast redwoods, giant sequoias, and numerous other tree species. You can visit the Camellia Grove and the Civil War Memorial Grove on the way to the Vietnam Veterans Memorial and the World Peace Rose Garden, which anchor the eastern end of the park.

Continue along the southern half of the park and meander west. Along the way you'll encounter the cactus garden and memorials to firefighters and veterans. Pass near the south steps of the capitol building and angle right (north) to the front of the capitol building, then cross Tenth Street, and return to the start of your capitol grounds walk, heading west between the California State Library and Court, now on your left, and the Jesse M. Unruh State Office Building on your right. You're now at the eastern end of Capitol Mall.

One of the iconic streets of downtown Sacramento, Capitol Mall passes government buildings, banks, and restaurants as it heads west. Occupying what would be M Street, Capitol Mall is divided by a green median, which is hugged by one-way vehicle traffic on each side. Walk west seven blocks from Ninth Street to Second Street, passing above I-5 between Second and Third Streets as the impressive visage of golden Tower Bridge juts above you.

Turn right on Second Street and follow it one block. You've now reached Old Sacramento, popular with both visitors and locals, where wooden boardwalks and restored buildings recreate the heart of the nineteenth-century city. Wander where you will among the restaurants and shops, but be sure to walk the paved path beside the Sacramento River, where you can't miss the *Delta King*, the 285-foot-long luxury steamboat that plied the waters between Sacramento and San Francisco from 1927 to 1940; it's now a hotel and restaurant.

Wend your way north to the museums and buildings of Old Sacramento State Historic Park. The park contains numerous buildings from the nineteenth century, including the California State Railroad Museum (open daily except Thanksgiving, Christmas, and New Year's Day). Learn more at www.californiarailroad.museum.

GO FARTHER

Cross the Tower Bridge from Old Sacramento to West Sacramento and immediately turn right into River Walk Park. This pleasant path travels through greenery and lets you drop right down to the banks of the Sacramento River, where you can watch birds flying about in front of Sacramento's downtown skyline. The path runs 0.3 mile past the multistepped Ziggurat office building to the I Street Bridge. Return the way you came, or cross the I Street Bridge and then turn right to drop back into Old Sacramento near the California State Railroad Museum.

3 William Land Park

DISTANCE:	3.0 miles of trails
ELEVATION GAIN:	Negligible
HIGH POINT:	15 feet
DIFFICULTY:	Easy
FITNESS:	Walkers, runners
FAMILY-FRIENDLY:	Yes, includes Sacramento Zoo and Fairytale Town
DOG-FRIENDLY:	On-leash
BIKE-FRIENDLY:	Yes
AMENITIES:	Bathrooms, picnic tables, water, wide variety of recreation facilities
CONTACT/MAP:	Sacramento City Parks and Recreation; download map from website
GPS:	N 38°32.349', W 121°30.137'
MORE KEY INFO:	Open sunrise to sunset; much of the park is wheelchair accessible

GETTING THERE

Driving: From downtown Sacramento, go south on I-5 for about 2.5 miles and take the Sutterville Road exit (exit 516), also signed for William Land Park and the Sacramento Zoo. Travel Sutterville Road for 0.4 mile and then turn left onto Land Park Drive. Continue another 0.1 mile and then park in the vicinity of the Sacramento Zoo and Fairytale Town. There are many other places in and near the park where you can park your car.

Transit: Bus 11 stops at several places in and near William Land Park, including at the Sacramento Zoo.

With everything you could possibly want in a suburban park—baseball diamonds, basketball courts, a golf course, a fishing pond, the Sacramento Zoo, Fairytale Town, numerous picnic tables, and an extensive road and trail system that lets you explore it all—William Land Park is popular with Sacramento residents of all ages and athletic proclivities. That said, it is a suburban park: a lot of people visit, and it's surrounded by busy streets, so it appeals most to those who want a nearby place to walk, and is especially suited for families with younger children.

GET MOVING

Rather than recommending a specific itinerary, this description provides general guidance and information and gives you the best options for enjoying William Land Park, a major destination for Sacramento residents since 1918. At 241 acres, the park is easy to navigate, and you shouldn't have any problem finding your way back to your parking spot. A network of roads and walking paths leads to all major parts of the park, and there are many places where you can leave the roads and paths to wander open grassy areas as well as under the shade of large trees.

Three main attractions await you in the southwest area of the park, near the parking area described in Getting There, above, and all have major appeal to the younger set. The Sacramento Zoo has nearly five hundred animals of many different species, from the big and tall—lions, snow leopards, and giraffes—to the small—aardvarks, meerkats, and reptiles. (Open daily except Christmas and Thanksgiving; see www.saczoo.org for more information, including admission fee.)

Fairytale Town delights young children with fairy-tale–themed play areas, farm animals, several gardens, and more. (Open daily except July 4, Thanksgiving, and Christmas; see www.fairytaletown.org for more information, including admission fee.)

Funderland has a variety of rides, giving young children the opportunity to fly on the back of a dragon, spin inside some really big cups, and ride the miniature train. (See http://funderlandpark.com for more information, including admission fee and hours.)

North of the Sacramento Zoo, Land Park Drive travels past Duck Lake a fishing spot where anglers young and old

Anne Rudin Peace Pond on the north side of William Land Park

try their luck. Farther along Land Park Drive several baseball diamonds make great stopping points during spring and summer if you want to catch a practice or a game.

A section of the park extends west from the northernmost baseball diamond, bounded by Riverside Boulevard, Eleventh Avenue, Thirteenth Avenue, and Thirteenth Street. This is a relatively peaceful area to meander among the large trees.

The northern boundary of the main part of the park lies along Thirteenth Avenue between Land Park Drive to the west and Freeport Boulevard to the east. Beautiful homes with interesting landscaping line the north side of Thirteenth Avenue, while on the south side in the park itself native trees such as redwoods, valley oaks, and California sycamores invite you to enjoy their cool shade. Be sure to visit the Anne

Rudin Peace Pond, accessed from Fourteenth Avenue to the north and Eighteenth Street to the east. Named for former Sacramento mayor Anne Rudin, the pond is a beautiful spot to watch ducks and geese.

You can also walk the perimeter of the park on the packed dirt path, which runs beside city streets with their attendant traffic noise. To have a more natural experience, in many instances you can walk a bit farther inside the park parallel to the packed dirt path.

Next page: *Oaks shade a section of the trail from Mormon Island Cove to Browns Ravine (Trail 11).*

GREATER SACRAMENTO URBAN AREA

The burgeoning population of the Sacramento area has expanded mainly eastward from downtown Sacramento, with small towns like Roseville and Folsom becoming sizable cities in recent decades. Indeed, much of the population of the greater urban area now lives outside of the Sacramento city limits.

The broad American River winds through this suburban expanse, and you'll find plenty of walking and hiking opportunities on and near this waterway. The Sacramento area is extremely fortunate to have the Jedediah Smith Memorial Trail (American River Bike Trail; see "The American River Parkway" sidebar in the Downtown Sacramento section), a paved path open to walkers and runners that stretches 32 miles along or near the American River from its confluence with the Sacramento River in Discovery Park all the way to Folsom Lake.

This section features several regional parks along the American River where you can both explore the Jedediah Smith Memorial Trail and wander dirt paths and roads that wind across the flood-plain and down to the banks of the river itself. You'll also find the best hikes farther upstream, including a long loop around Lake Natoma, plus paths running along and above the shores of Folsom Lake. Two hikes also run along the riparian corridor of Dry Creek in the Roseville area.

4

Gibson Ranch Regional Park

DISTANCE·	2.6-mile loop
ELEVATION GAIN:	Negligible
HIGH POINT:	90 feet
DIFFICULTY:	Easy
FITNESS:	Walkers, runners
FAMILY-FRIENDLY:	Yes, Gibson Lake playground
DOG-FRIENDLY:	On-leash
BIKE-FRIENDLY:	No
AMENITIES:	Bathroom, picnic tables, playground, and drinking fountains on north side of Gibson Lake
CONTACT/MAP:	Sacramento County Regional Parks; no map
GPS:	N 38˚43.721', W 121˚23.951'
MORE KEY INFO:	Open sunrise to a half hour before sunset; fee; do not feed the animals

GETTING THERE

Driving: Take the Watt Avenue exit about 8 miles from downtown Sacramento either via I-80 (exit 94A) or Business 80/Capitol City Freeway (exit 14B). Drive Watt Avenue for 5.8 miles north of I-80 and then turn left onto Elverta Road. Continue 0.9 mile and then turn right onto Gibson Ranch Park Road and into Gibson Ranch Regional Park. Go north 0.7 mile to a stop sign. Continue north and then swing east around Gibson Lake. Continue straight at another stop sign at 1.3 miles and then park in the dirt lot on the left at 1.7 miles, across the road from group picnic site 3D.

Transit: Bus 19 stops on Watt Avenue at Elverta Road. Walk Elverta Road for 0.9 mile, turn right into Gibson Ranch Regional Park, and then walk 0.3 mile along the park road to join the hike in the clockwise direction at the 1.2-mile mark.

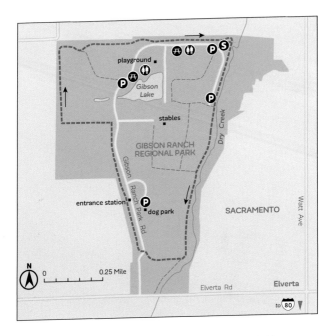

Make no mistake about it: This is a working ranch with numerous farm animals, including some magnificent horses that you'll see up close. But Gibson Ranch Regional Park also offers natural areas, especially along Dry Creek, and opportunities for distant views of the Coast Range and Sierra Nevada. It's especially appealing to families, who can enjoy the playground and picnic area at Gibson Lake after their hike.

GET MOVING

Head for the trail sign and the dirt road (the trail) on the far side of the parking lot near a yellow post on the north side of the park. Begin walking east under the shade of larger valley oaks and smaller blue oaks, varieties of trees that you'll see for the initial portion of the journey near Dry Creek. After 100 yards the route swings 90 degrees south and allows the first view of Dry Creek to your left (east).

Proceed south along a levee that protects Gibson Ranch from inundation when winter and spring storms swell Dry Creek. Contrary to its name, Dry Creek is a year-round stream that begins in the Sierra Nevada foothills of Placer County and gently winds its way to a meeting with the Sacramento River near its confluence with the American River.

This stretch along the west side of Dry Creek has the most natural beauty of the entire hike. Yes, the park road is just to your right, with picnic areas adjacent and ranchlands beyond, but the lush green of streamside cottonwoods, willows, and other water-loving plants will draw most of your attention. A few side paths lead streamside, giving the opportunity to sit still and observe the many bird species that call this area home.

Continue under oak shade and past an understory that has a mix of native and nonnative species. (Look for nonnative fennel with its needle-thin leaves that smell and taste like licorice.) At 0.5 mile briefly leave the levee to detour around a fallen valley oak that is still alive, and then rejoin the levee 100 feet farther. Stay straight on the levee when a dirt road comes in on the right at 0.6 mile.

You'll see and hear traffic on busy Elverta Road just before you leave Dry Creek at 1.0 mile to turn right on a dirt road. Walk west; you'll see a pasture on the right and an oak-shaded ditch on the left. Meet the main park road at 1.2 miles. Cross it and turn right to walk north on a narrow path that parallels the main park road. This is the least interesting part of the hike, but persevere as you pass the entrance station and a dog park to reach a stop sign at 1.6 miles.

Go left (west) on a broad dirt road, marked by a "Pasture 16" sign. The way now passes through a slice of rural ranch life, with horses pastured on both sides of the road. Reach the western boundary of Gibson Ranch Regional Park at 1.9 miles,

Dry Creek adds riparian beauty to Gibson Ranch Regional Park.

where the dirt road turns north. This is the best spot to spy the hills and low mountains of the Coast Range lining the far western edge of the Sacramento Valley. Also look east at the blue expanse of the Sierra Nevada, snowcapped for much of the year.

Wander under oak shade past marshes and wetlands frequented by herons, egrets, and red-winged blackbirds to the northwest boundary of the park at 2.1 miles, where you turn right and walk east. You'll encounter a dirt road on the right after 100 feet; take it if you want to go straight to Gibson Lake. The hike continues due east on the dirt road beside the northern boundary.

Enjoy open views of ranchland and the Sierra Nevada as you continue. At 2.4 miles you'll see the main park road and the green expanse surrounding Gibson Lake on the right. Continue straight another 0.2 mile to the trailhead to complete the 2.6-mile loop.

GO FARTHER

Gibson Lake features picnic tables, a children's playground, and restrooms. You can wander along the water's edge and throughout the green expanse bordering the lake and extending north to the main park road.

5 Dry Creek Greenway

DISTANCE:	2.8 miles roundtrip
ELEVATION GAIN:	Negligible
HIGH POINT:	100 feet
DIFFICULTY:	Easy
FITNESS:	Walkers, runners
FAMILY-FRIENDLY:	Yes, playground at trailhead
DOG-FRIENDLY:	On-leash
BIKE-FRIENDLY:	Yes
AMENITIES:	Bathrooms, picnic tables, water at trailhead
CONTACT/MAP:	Placer County Parks and Trails; no map online
GPS:	N 38°44.069', W 121°21.793'
MORE KEY INFO:	Open a half hour before sunrise to a half hour after sunset; wheelchair accessible

GETTING THERE

Driving: From downtown Sacramento, follow I-80 northeast about 12 miles, and take the Elkhorn Boulevard exit (exit 98). Go left (west) on Elkhorn Boulevard (or right, if coming the opposite direction on I-80) 1.8 miles, and then turn right (north) on Walerga Road. Continue 2.7 miles on Walerga Road and turn right into Dry Creek Community Park.

This greenway in Roseville appeals most to people looking for an easy walking path that combines accessibility with the natural beauty of Dry Creek and its bordering grasslands. It is an especially good outing if you have kids: there's a

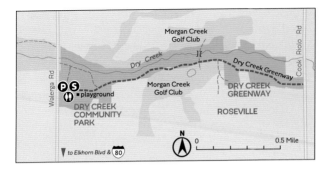

playground at the trailhead and the paved path is perfect for pushing a stroller.

GET MOVING

Start your walk or run near the restrooms. Pause at the informational kiosk to read about the natural and human history of Dry Creek and about the ongoing plans to create a 30-mile-long trail network for walkers, runners, and cyclists.

If you have young kids with you, they will likely make a bee-line for the children's playground, a circular area just beyond the bathrooms. Other recreational facilities include tennis courts, a basketball court, and baseball and soccer fields.

Take the paved path on the right (south) as you walk east from the parking lot. Continue past the baseball and soccer fields to a junction at 0.2 mile. The left-hand route is described in Go Farther, below; turn right for the main part of the hike.

You'll immediately spot the dirt path on the left that parallels the paved path. The dirt path usually stays close to the paved path, but it also curves away at times to wander through a dense greenery of valley oaks, black walnut trees, interior live oaks, blackberry bushes, and California wild grape. Numerous side paths quickly lead to the banks of Dry Creek. The stream is definitely misnamed: it flows year-round from its source in the Sierra Nevada foothills down to the Sacramento River.

Natural beauty now becomes more prominent as you leave the manicured civilization of Dry Creek Community Park. Cottonwoods, willows, and other riparian vegetation border unseen Dry Creek on the left, and you pass through open grasslands that bloom with a variety of wildflowers from early spring into midsummer. You'll see homes and a horse pasture on the right at 0.3 mile followed shortly thereafter by the close-cropped greenery of the Morgan Creek Golf Club.

Tall valley oaks border parts of the trail, providing welcome shade on warm days. At 0.9 mile a paved path heads

The Dry Creek Greenway is popular with runners and families.

left to cross Dry Creek on a bridge. You may be tempted to walk the bridge to get a good view of Dry Creek, but be on the lookout for golf cart traffic since the bridge links the two main parts of the Morgan Creek Golf Club course.

At 1.0 mile the route passes under powerlines and leaves the golf course behind. You now pass through open grasslands dotted with young valley oak trees to reach the turnaround point at 1.4 miles at Cook Riolo Road. From here, retrace your steps to the trailhead.

GO FARTHER
The paved Dry Creek Greenway path continues west from Walerga Road for a half mile. To reach it, turn left at the trail junction encountered at 0.2 mile or take the short connecter path north from the west end of the Dry Creek Community Park parking lot to the meeting of the Dry Creek Greenway path and Walerga Road. Carefully cross Walerga Road, then proceed north 100 yards to find the path on your left.

6 Mather Regional Park

DISTANCE:	1.6 miles roundtrip
ELEVATION GAIN:	Negligible
HIGH POINT:	145 feet
DIFFICULTY:	Easy
FITNESS:	Walkers
FAMILY-FRIENDLY:	Yes, large playground at trailhead
DOG-FRIENDLY:	On-leash
BIKE-FRIENDLY:	No
AMENITIES:	Bathrooms, picnic tables, water
CONTACT/MAP:	Sacramento County Regional Parks; download map from website
GPS:	N 38°33.418', W 121°15.578'
MORE KEY INFO:	Open sunrise to sunset daily; fee

GETTING THERE

Driving: From downtown Sacramento, drive about 17 miles east on US Highway 50. Take the Zinfandel Drive exit (exit 17). Turn right (south) onto Zinfandel Drive. (If driving west on US 50 toward I-5 and downtown Sacramento, turn left onto Zinfandel Avenue.) Follow Zinfandel Drive south for 2.8 miles and then turn left at the sign for Mather Regional Park (0.2 mile south of Douglas Road). Parking is on your left.

More and more local residents are discovering Mather Regional Park, making it popular with families and people who love to fish. Mather Lake itself is the main draw, and both trails in the park take you near the shore. Both also explore the open grasslands, with the shorter nature trail offering ten interpretive signs that explain the area's natural history.

GET MOVING

Walk past the entrance-fee pay station and through the center of the grass lawn and by numerous picnic tables to the edge of Mather Lake where you'll likely be greeted by Canada geese. You're standing on what once was Mather Air Force Base, an extensive military installation that was a major air base for B-52 bombers. The base was closed in 1993 after the end of the Cold War. The land has reverted to civilian use, paving the way for the creation of popular Mather Regional Park.

The blue expanse of willow- and cottonwood-ringed Mather Lake stretches east. Created when the air force dammed Morrison Creek, the lake is a permanent home to many birds, including great blue herons, egrets, blackbirds, Canada geese, and mallard ducks, and in winter and spring it hosts substantial numbers of migrating waterbirds. The California Department of Fish and Game stocks the lake with channel catfish and rainbow trout, so you'll see anglers along the shoreline.

A peaceful, sunny day at Mather Lake Regional Park

To begin the nature trail (0.4 mile roundtrip), walk near the lakeshore on a dirt road, heading north and staying to the right near the shore when another dirt road (the return route) branches left. Enjoy views between willows and cottonwoods, then turn left at 0.1 mile and enter open grasslands dotted by small valley oaks and numerous coyote bushes. You'll certainly spot resident ground squirrels, and perhaps even a desert cottontail or jackrabbit. You'll soon reach the first of ten signs about local flora and fauna.

Continue to the last of the signs near the northernmost point of the trail, close to Douglas Road. Look for the continuation of the loop on the left. You may want to return the way you came. To complete the loop, follow it south past valley oaks and vernal pools that bloom briefly with a rainbow of wildflowers in late spring. Reach the lakeshore near the

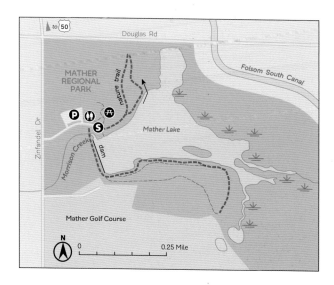

beginning of the trail by the main park at 0.4 mile, then follow
the lakeshore back to the green lawn.

For the longer hike in Mather Regional Park (1.2 miles
roundtrip), walk to the dam, which is just south of the parking
lot. Cross the dam and go south on the paved path for 0.1
mile to the southwest edge of Mather Lake. Leave the pavement here and take the dirt path that runs near the southern
shore of the lake. There are actually two main parallel trails:
One is narrower and closer to the water but with much better
views of the lake; the other, farther away from the water, offers
easier walking. Stay on the one by the lake until it gets narrow,
and then walk briefly to your right to join the broader trail.

At 0.5 mile the main path swings south, with tules and
cattails on the left and a lot of coyote bush to the right. At
0.6 mile the trail nears Mather Golf Course. The surest bet is
to return the way you came to the parking lot. If you're feel-
ing more adventurous, follow the faint continuation of the

trail westerly across the open grasslands to a dirt road that runs west to meet the paved trail you initially walked on after crossing the dam. Be forewarned that you'll occasionally have to walk through flowers and grasses, so this is definitely not the best option from late spring onward when the vegetation is dry and full of stickers.

7 William B. Pond Recreation Area

DISTANCE:	Up to 2.0 miles of trails
ELEVATION GAIN:	Negligible
HIGH POINT:	50 feet
DIFFICULTY:	Easy
FITNESS:	Walkers, runners
FAMILY-FRIENDLY:	Yes
DOG-FRIENDLY:	On-leash; not allowed in nature study area
BIKE-FRIENDLY:	Yes, only on Jedediah Smith Memorial Trail
AMENITIES:	Bathrooms, picnic tables, and water fountains located in both parks
CONTACT/MAP:	Sacramento County Regional Parks; download map from website
GPS:	N 38°35.282', W 121°20.091'
MORE KEY INFO:	Open sunrise to sunset daily; fee; fishing pond; paved paths are wheelchair accessible

GETTING THERE

Driving: Drive US Highway 50 from downtown Sacramento about 11 miles and then take the Watt Avenue exit (exit 11). Go left (north; go right if coming from the other direction on US 50) and drive Watt Avenue north for 1.2 miles. Turn right on Fair Oaks Boulevard, go 2.5 miles, and then turn right on Arden Way. Follow Arden Way 0.7 mile to William B. Pond Recreation Area, then park in the large lot on the left that is 200 yards past the pay station.

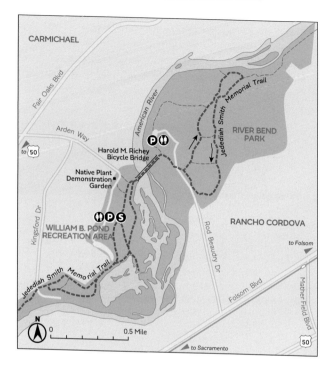

This recreation area and park lie on opposite sides of the American River. Each offers a variety of walking and recreational opportunities, with the American River as the highlight. The Jedediah Smith Memorial Trail (American River Bike Trail; see "The American River Parkway" sidebar in the Downtown Sacramento section) links the two via the Harold M. Richey Bicycle Bridge. Together, the two parks are a perfect spot to bring the kids, enjoy a picnic, and wander through the natural beauty.

GET MOVING

Walking opportunities abound in these two parks, so this description doesn't give a detailed itinerary but rather presents the main options, allowing you to choose what suits you and your hiking companions.

Like to fish? Don't fish but love ponds? Then head past the restrooms, and either turn right on the paved Jedediah Smith Memorial Trail or cross the Jedediah Smith Memorial Trail to reach a dirt path on the far side. Either will bring you to the shoreline of the fishing pond, a beautiful spot to watch anglers young and old trying their luck, or to just watch the waterfowl enjoying the calm water.

Consider continuing along the path on the northwest shore of the pond and beyond to eventually either return the way you came to the parking area or take the adjacent Jedediah Smith Memorial Trail instead, which allows you to return to the parking area or go southwest. Remember: When on the Jedediah Smith Memorial Trail, take care to walk or run on the left side facing oncoming bicycle traffic.

Back near the parking area, wander under the shade of mature California sycamores and valley oaks and past picnic tables to the pay station. From there, cross the street to the Native Plant Demonstration Garden, adjacent to the American River Parkway Foundation Volunteer Center.

A network of paths leads through the six major areas of the Native Plant Demonstration Garden, each with a distinctive association of plant species. Zone 1, the Audubon Area, features plants that attract foraging birds. Zone 2, Pollinator Paradise, has blooming plants that attract bees and butterflies. Zone 3, Lilac Grove, contains Ceanothus species. Zone 4, Redbud Forest, has redbuds and native groundcover. Zone 5, Scrub Understory, highlights native plants that grow under oak trees. Zone 6, Manzanita Area, has various specimens of manzanita.

Now head toward the river to catch the Jedediah Smith Memorial Trail and turn left (north) to cross the river on the Harold M. Richey Bicycle Bridge. Cross carefully while watching for cyclists, but be sure to pause in the middle to

Sycamores shade a grassy expanse in William B. Pond Recreation Area.

see the broad American River flow below. Cottonwoods and willows line the banks on both sides and in both directions, and numerous vegetated islands break up the flow on the downstream side of the bridge. You'll certainly see swallows flitting about, and you may also spy a great blue heron or a flock of Canada geese.

River Bend Park awaits on the far side of the bridge. The land here was first acquired in the early 1960s, making it one of Sacramento County's oldest parks. Immediately on the left a paved path drops to an extensive picnic area with a restroom and drinking fountain, with ample shade from live oaks and valley oaks. From here you can access a network of informal trails that allows exploration near and along the riverbank upstream of the bridge; you'll find many peaceful and secluded spots to just sit and watch the water glide by.

Continuing on the Jedediah Smith Memorial Trail near the bridge, you'll soon cross Rod Beaudry Drive. Look for a broad dirt trail on the left just 100 feet beyond. (Note: Since the path traverses a designated nature study area, dogs are not allowed, even on leash.) This trail, crossed by several lesser paths, runs north 0.4 mile to the banks of the American River, alternating between valley oak shade and open areas flush with wildflowers in spring.

From the river you can return the way you came, following the dirt path back to the Jedediah Smith Memorial Trail near the bridge, or continue another 0.1 mile to catch the Jedediah Smith Memorial Trail and then head back to the bridge. Cross the bridge to return to the trailhead in William B. Pond Recreation Area.

GO FARTHER

You can walk as far as you want in either direction on the Jedediah Smith Memorial Trail. Both options are quite beautiful and take you past riparian vegetation near the American River and through upland oak vegetation farther away from the riverbanks.

8 Effie Yeaw Nature Center Loop

DISTANCE:	1.3-mile loop
ELEVATION GAIN:	50 feet
HIGH POINT:	80 feet
DIFFICULTY:	Easy
FITNESS:	Walkers, hikers
FAMILY-FRIENDLY:	Yes; Nature Center has many exhibits kids will love; river access
DOG-FRIENDLY:	No
BIKE-FRIENDLY:	No
AMENITIES:	Bathrooms, water
CONTACT/MAP:	Sacramento County Regional Parks; map online: Ancil Hoffman Park
GPS:	N 38°37.004', W 121°18.749'
MORE KEY INFO:	Trails open dawn to dusk; park fee; Nature Center (free, donations encouraged) open Tues.–Sun.; check website for hours

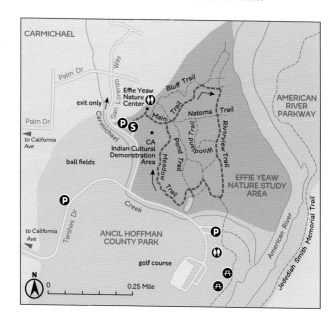

GETTING THERE

Driving: Drive US Highway 50 from downtown Sacramento about 11 miles and then take the Watt Avenue exit (exit 11). Go left (right if coming from the other direction on US 50) and drive Watt Avenue north for 1.2 miles. Turn right on Fair Oaks Boulevard, and at 4.0 miles, turn right again on Van Alstine Avenue. Go 0.4 mile, turn left on California Avenue, and then, after 0.1 mile, turn right on Tarshes Drive (you'll soon enter Ancil Hoffman County Park). Following signs for Effie Yeaw Nature Center, go 0.7 mile to San Lorenzo Way and turn left. Find the large parking lot on the right in 0.2 mile.

Transit: Bus 23 stops on Fair Oaks Boulevard at El Camino Avenue. Walk 0.4 mile on Van Alstine Avenue, turn left on California Avenue to the intersection with Tarshes Drive, and then turn right and follow the driving directions above for a total of 1.4 miles.

Located in Ancil Hoffman County Park, the Effie Yeaw Nature Center and associated trails are a quiet respite in the natural world from the bustle of Sacramento-area urban life. Here you and your family can learn about local human and natural history and also visit a variety of habitats: woodlands, meadows, ponds, and the banks of the American River.

GET MOVING

From the parking lot, follow signs for the Effie Yeaw Nature Center past an observation pond and a variety of native plants, many with identifying signs. Immediately reach the California Indian Cultural Demonstration Area, where you'll find details about the culture and way of life of the Valley Nisenan. You can view reconstructions of tule huts, an acorn granary, and much more, all clearly explained with interpretive signage.

Children explore the banks of the American River.

EFFIE YEAW

Can one person really make a difference? The answer is yes, and the life of Effie Yeaw proves it. In 1955, the local teacher began leading groups of schoolchildren through the oak forests and open meadows near the American River in an area of Carmichael then known as Deterding Woods. She taught the students about cultural history and plants, animals, reptiles, insects, and ecological relationships. Her inspiration and dedication lies behind the many educational programs and displays at the Effie Yeaw Nature Center, as well as the many interconnected trails in the area.

Yeaw was a key member of the Save the American River Association and a major force behind the creation of the American River Parkway. Several parks and trail systems featured in this book, including the Jedediah Smith Memorial Trail, are in this parkway. When she passed away in 1970, Yeaw left the Greater Sacramento area a lasting legacy, a devotion to environmental education and conservation that will continue to benefit the region for years to come.

The Effie Yeaw Nature Center waits just beyond and is well worth your time. Honoring teacher, conservationist, and environmental educator Effie Yeaw (see "Effie Yeaw" sidebar), the nonprofit Nature Center contains a variety of informative displays about the lower American River, including its flora, fauna, and cultural history. It also cares for numerous non-releasable animals that can't survive in the wild; view a great horned owl, a peregrine falcon, a Swainson's hawk, and many other birds, plus an assortment of amphibians and reptiles, including a rattlesnake. Entrance is free, but donations are encouraged.

To start the recommended hike, look for the beginning of the trail between the Effie Yeaw Nature Center and the California Indian Cultural Demonstration Area. There are many trail forks on the hike described here, but most are well signed and it's hard to get lost for long in the 100-acre expanse; in addition, signs direct you back to the Effie Yeaw Nature Center. Note that you are required to stay on trails.

Start on the Main Trail. Over the first 0.1 mile it quickly meets three narrow trails: first the Meadow Trail (the return route), then the Pond Trail, and then the Natoma Trail. Stay on the Main Trail as it curves left and passes through oak woodlands dotted with interior live oak, blue oak, and valley oak.

Stay right at an intersection with the Bluff Trail at 0.2 mile as you get the first good view of the American River. Almost immediately, take the next trail on the right to reach the Riverview Trail. Turn right again and follow the Riverview Trail in the downstream direction of the American River under the partial shade of mature valley oaks and past streamside willows and cottonwoods. Several side paths allow you to access the riverbank. You'll definitely want to spend time quietly watching the water flow by, and you'll likely spot great blue herons, Canada geese, mallard ducks, and other water-loving birds.

Cross the Natoma Trail at 0.4 mile, stay straight when the Woodland Trail comes in on the right, and then pass between several buckeye trees at 0.5 mile. Stay straight again at the next trail junction, continuing to parallel the river on the Riverview Trail until you reach a junction at 0.7 mile. Take the path on the right signed for the Pond Trail, to another junction at 0.8 mile with the Meadow Trail. Briefly head left to visit the nearby pond, a tranquil spot to pause and enjoy the lush vegetation and variety of birds, insects, and other creatures.

Back at the previously encountered junction, take the Meadow Trail through an interior live oak forest with an understory of nonnative Himalaya blackberry. At 0.9 mile valley oaks predominate, festooned with California wild grapevines growing as high as forty feet up trunks and along branches. At 1.1 miles pass a blue elderberry and some black walnut trees before bordering a broad meadow that, in spring, blooms with lupine, vetch, and other wildflowers. Reach the Main Trail at nearly 1.3 miles. Turn left and you'll soon be back at the Effie Yeaw Nature Center where you began the hike.

GO FARTHER

There's another mile-plus of trails within the Effie Yeaw Nature Center area; the lollipop loop described above intersects most of them.

9　Sacramento Bar

DISTANCE:	Up to 8.0 miles of trails
ELEVATION GAIN:	Up to 100 feet
HIGH POINT:	95 feet
DIFFICULTY:	Easy
FITNESS:	Walkers, hikers, runners
FAMILY-FRIENDLY:	Yes
DOG-FRIENDLY:	On-leash
BIKE-FRIENDLY:	Yes, on paved trails only
AMENITIES:	Bathrooms, picnic tables, and water fountains in both parks
CONTACT/MAP:	Sacramento County Regional Parks; download map from website
GPS:	N 38˚38.001', W 121˚16.376'
MORE KEY INFO:	Open sunrise to sunset daily; fee; paved paths are wheelchair accessible

GETTING THERE

Driving: Head east on US Highway 50 about 17 miles from downtown Sacramento and take the Sunrise Boulevard exit (exit 18). Go north 2.4 miles on Sunrise Boulevard (crossing the American River), then turn left (west) on Fair Oaks Boulevard. Go 0.1 mile and turn left (south) onto Pennsylvania Avenue, which you take for 0.4 mile to the entrance of Sacramento Bar Regional Park. Continue past the entrance station to the large parking lot just beyond, parking closest to the river.

Transit: You can get off Bus 21 at two locations close to the park. If you take the Fair Oaks Boulevard stop, follow Fair Oaks Boulevard 0.1 mile west then turn left on Pennsylvania Avenue and walk 0.4 mile into Sacramento Bar Regional Park. If you use the Sunrise Boulevard at Gold Country Boulevard stop, cross Sunrise Boulevard, walk north toward the river, then take South Bridge Street into the Lower Sunrise Recreation Area, 0.2 mile total.

These two Sacramento County parks, across the American River from one another and joined by the Jim Jones Bridge, have a lot to offer, including plenty of opportunities to explore the river, wander among several ponds, and enjoy a variety of riparian and foothill plant life as well as an aerial assortment of birds, including geese and ducks.

GET MOVING

This description presents several options for your exploration but doesn't provide detailed, step-by-step instructions since there's a lot to see and do via a myriad of interconnected dirt trails, dirt roads, paved bike paths (primarily the Jedediah Smith Memorial Trail), and paved park roads. Although the book map offers an overview, make sure you download the park PDF map before your visit; you'll definitely want it if you plan to explore Sacramento Bar and its environs in detail.

You have two main options in Sacramento Bar Regional Park. The first features access to the bank of the American River and the opportunity to visit the ponds nestled into a crook in the river. From the parking lot, head toward the river by turning right on a paved bike path. (Note: This is not the Jedediah Smith Memorial Trail, which is on the other side of the river and is described in the Lower Sunrise Recreation Area options below.) Continuing on the bike path is the second option, but for now go 200 feet or so under blue oak shade, take the first good dirt trail on the left, and follow it toward the river.

You quickly reach a wide gravel road (a fire road) that parallels the American River. Turn right and follow this road in the downstream direction, passing cottonwoods and willows and numerous opportunities to access the riverbank for a swim or to just watch the water (and rafters and kayakers) flow by.

After 0.7 mile, the gravel road curves right and westerly, away from the river, and soon bisects two large ponds. Stop to explore the nearer one on the left; it's a perfect spot to watch geese and ducks flying above the water and swimming the surface. Be sure to listen for the trill of red-winged blackbirds. This is a good point to turn around and head back to the parking area. However, you can follow the dirt road as it swings north 0.4 mile to end near the playing field of the Waldorf School. Some rough and overgrown trails connect to the

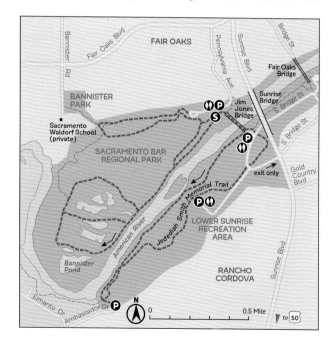

Rafters launch on the American River at Lower Sunrise Recreation Area.

paved bike path described below, but they are not easy to find or navigate, and there is no signage to guide you.

For the second Sacramento Bar Regional Park hiking option, leave from the parking area and head toward the river, turning right on the paved bike path. In contrast to the first option, stay on this paved bike path as it runs west 1.0 mile through oak woodlands to end at Bannister Park beside the Sacramento Waldorf School. If you'd prefer not to walk or run on a paved path, you'll find a dirt path that parallels the bike route; find it 0.1 mile from the trailhead where the bike path makes a pronounced arc. Return to the parking lot from Bannister Park the way you came.

To explore Lower Sunrise Recreation Area, begin at the parking lot in Sacramento Bar Regional Park. Walk to the paved bike path and turn left, soon crossing the American River on the Jim Jones Bridge. Pause midway to watch the river coursing below your feet and to get a bird's-eye view of people launching watercraft just below the bridge. (Lower Sunrise Recreation Area is a major put-in point for both commercial rafting companies and private parties.) You'll definitely hear traffic from nearby Sunrise Boulevard when you're on the bridge, but the noise fades considerably once you're on the southern bank of the river.

Drop down to just past the bridge in the Lower Sunrise Recreation Area. Walk past the boat launch area just beside the river to find a wide dirt path that runs west and downstream along the south bank of the American River. Follow this path for a long mile, enjoying the shade of cottonwoods and willows and the many opportunities to access the river. The path eventually crosses the Jedediah Smith Memorial Trail (American River Bike Trail; see "The American River Parkway" sidebar in the Downtown Sacramento section) to end at a parking area at the edge of a residential area.

To return to the Jim Jones Bridge and the trailhead in Sacramento Bar Park, either return upstream the way you just came, or opt for a longer walk on the Jedediah Smith Memorial Trail. Just turn left when you meet it and then follow it easterly 1.4 miles back to the big parking lot in Lower Sunrise Recreation Area, within sight of the Jim Jones Bridge. From here, cross the river via the Jim Jones Bridge to Sacramento Bar Regional Park and the parking area.

GO FARTHER

You can walk or run on the Jedediah Smith Memorial Trail in either direction for any length, returning the way you came.

10 Lake Natoma Loop

DISTANCE:	10.9-mile loop
ELEVATION GAIN:	400 feet
HIGH POINT:	180 feet
DIFFICULTY:	Moderate
FITNESS:	Walkers, runners
FAMILY-FRIENDLY:	Yes
DOG-FRIENDLY:	On-leash
BIKE-FRIENDLY:	Yes
AMENITIES:	Bathrooms, picnic tables, and water at trailhead and along route; bring plenty of water
CONTACT/MAP:	Folsom Lake State Recreation Area; download map from website but also available at entrance station
GPS:	N 38°38.200', W 121°12.826'
MORE KEY INFO:	Open 6 AM to 9 PM during Daylight Saving Time, 7 AM to 7 PM, rest of year; fee

GETTING THERE

Driving: On US Highway 50, drive about 20 miles from downtown Sacramento to the Hazel Avenue exit (exit 21). Turn left (north) on Hazel Avenue, which crosses over US 50. Go 200 yards, cross Tributary Point Drive, and then immediately take the next right signed for Nimbus Flat, Lake Natoma Unit, and Folsom SRA (state recreation area). Pass the entrance station, follow the road 0.2 mile, and then turn right to reach a large parking lot for the picnic area. The trail begins near the far corner of the lot near the restrooms.

Transit: The Light Rail Gold Line stops at Hazel Station. Walk Folsom Boulevard 200 yards southwest, turn right on Hazel Avenue, and continue across US 50 (on an overpass) for another 300 yards (see driving directions above).

Very popular with cyclists, the Lake Natoma Loop also offers a lot for walkers and runners. The paved route passes through foothill woodlands and near riparian areas along Lake Natoma

FLOOD CONTROL IN
THE SACRAMENTO AREA

Many rivers flow out of the Sierra Nevada, including the American River, which runs east to west across Sacramento County. However, winter and spring rains historically inundated the Central Valley, including catastrophic floods in Sacramento in the winter of 1861–62.

The federal government has assumed primary responsibility for flood control in the state. Inaugurated in the 1930s, the Central Valley Project incorporates major dams to the north, including the Shasta Dam across the Sacramento River, plus Folsom and Nimbus Dams on the American River in Sacramento County, along with many other dams throughout the Sierra Nevada. These dams regulate the river flow to prevent flooding, provide irrigation water to the many productive farms in the Central Valley, generate electricity for much of the state, and create recreational opportunities for residents and visitors on and near their impounded reservoirs, like Folsom Lake. Along with these benefits, the dams and water diversion have created substantial environmental problems that continue to be controversial.

Many of the trails described in this book take place on lands affected by the Central Valley Project and similar projects. You may spot some levees running parallel to rivers and streams; they are designed to contain floodwater. Some routes, like the Putah Creek Riparian Reserve just south of Davis, run across levees.

and its tributary streams, with options to walk on bordering dirt paths. Yes, parts of the trail pass through suburban areas, but much of it is also natural and peaceful. Interpretive signs explain the human and natural history of the area.

GET MOVING

Find the trail beyond the bathrooms near the southeast corner of the parking lot. Follow it 0.2 mile to a paved road. Turn left and follow the paved road for 0.1 mile, then leave the paved road to turn right onto the paved South Lake Natoma Bike Path. Head northerly and start a counterclockwise

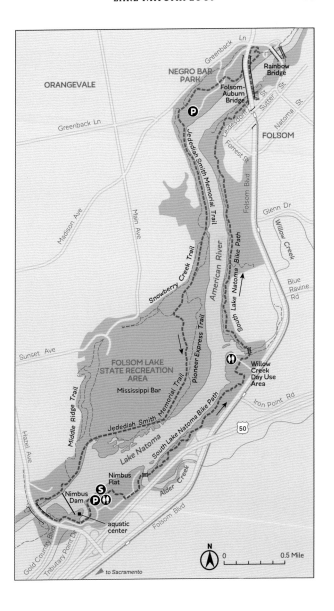

journey around Lake Natoma. Completed in 1955, Nimbus Dam impounds the waters of the lower American River to create the lake. The dam and lake are part of the Central Valley Project, which was designed to provide irrigation water, drinking water, flood control, electricity, and recreational opportunities for California's Central Valley (see "Flood Control in the Sacramento Area" sidebar).

Walkers and runners should use the dirt trail on the left side of the South Lake Natoma Bike Path, facing oncoming bike traffic. This is important for your safety and for that of cyclists. As you continue your excursion, you'll see numerous opportunities to use dirt trails that travel closer to the lakeshore. Feel free to explore, making sure you always know how to get back to the paved path. Various access paths come in from nearby neighborhoods; pay attention to signs to ensure that you stay on the South Lake Natoma Bike Path.

At 0.6 mile the trail crosses Alder Creek on a bridge where you'll have a good view of Lake Natoma and a variety of sailboats, sculls, and other watercraft. As you continue, traffic noise from US 50 soon fades, although you may still hear lesser noise from Folsom Boulevard. The route travels through typical Sierra foothill vegetation: Blue oak, interior live oak, and gray pine are the main tree species, with an understory of buckbrush, toyon, whiteleaf manzanita, and coyote bush. Wildflowers are prominent in spring.

Reach the Willow Creek Day Use Area at 2.2 miles (bathrooms and drinking fountains available). Beyond Willow Creek the route veers away from Folsom Boulevard toward the lake into a quieter milieu. After passing commercial buildings, enter an open area at 2.9 miles filled with dredge tailings from the American River's gold rush days of the mid-nineteenth century. The next mile is quite peaceful with good opportunities to explore along the lakeshore using the dirt path that borders the South Lake Natoma Bike Path.

Sailing and kayaking are popular activities on Lake Natoma.

The trail goes under the Folsom-Auburn Bridge at 4.7 miles; look for steps on the other side that lead up to the bridge itself. Cross Lake Natoma using the pedestrian section of the bridge and stop to gaze at the lake and to admire historic Rainbow Bridge (built in 1918) just to the east. Now on the other side of the lake, turn right on Greenback Lane and then immediately turn right again onto a paved path to descend and rejoin the paved path. Now that you're on the northwest side of Lake Natoma, you begin the southerly part of the journey.

Follow signs for Negro Bar Park, pass under the Folsom-Auburn Bridge, and then, at 5.0 miles, enter Negro Bar Park; Negro Bar was named for the African American miners who first prospected for gold here in 1850. Your paved path is now the Jedediah Smith Memorial Trail (American River Bike Trail; see "The American River Parkway" sidebar in the Downtown Sacramento section). Cross a parking lot to stay on the main paved bike path as you pass restrooms, picnic tables, and drinking fountains. At 5.9 miles the path meets the Pioneer Express Trail. This dirt trail (for hikers and equestrians only) continues most of the way to Nimbus Dam and Hazel Avenue and is a good alternate to the main paved route described here.

Cliffs soon force the Jedediah Smith Memorial Trail to run near the shoreline, allowing good views of Lake Natoma. At 6.9 miles the route moves away from Lake Natoma to climb into the Mississippi Bar area. Wander through the open grasslands dotted with blue oaks and interior live oaks, where you'll enjoy wildflowers in spring.

At 9.4 miles the Pioneer Express Trail merges with the main paved trail. Nimbus Dam and the western terminus of Lake Natoma are now in plain sight. Walk or run past Nimbus Dam and then climb the short trail up to the Hazel Avenue Bridge at 9.9 miles. Turn left and follow the bridge across the American River.

At the end of the Hazel Avenue Bridge, turn left at 10.1 miles on the paved trail. It travels beside Hazel Avenue and then borders the Sacramento State Aquatic Center. Just beyond, it crosses the main access road to the Nimbus Flat portion of Folsom Lake SRA, just east of the pay station.

You can follow the road 0.3 mile to your vehicle. If you stay on the path, walk a half mile and then turn left at the previously encountered junction to return to the trailhead at 10.9 miles.

Mormon Island Cove to Browns Ravine

11

DISTANCE:	4.8 miles roundtrip
ELEVATION GAIN:	350 feet
HIGH POINT:	550 feet
DIFFICULTY:	Easy to moderate
FITNESS:	Hikers, runners
FAMILY-FRIENDLY:	Yes, but watch for poison oak
DOG-FRIENDLY:	On-leash
BIKE-FRIENDLY:	Yes
AMENITIES:	None
CONTACT/MAP:	Folsom Lake State Recreation Area; download map from website or use brochure map
GPS:	N 38˚42.100', W 121˚6.591'
MORE KEY INFO:	Open daily 7 AM to 9 PM during Daylight Saving Time, 7 AM to 6 PM rest of year; fee; watch for mountain bikers; powerboat noise in summer

GETTING THERE

Driving: Drive US Highway 50 east from downtown Sacramento about 27 miles and take the East Bidwell Street exit (exit 27). Go left (right if coming from the other direction on US 50), and at 0.2 mile turn right on Iron Point Road. After 1.7 miles turn left onto Empire Ranch Road. Go another 1.7 miles and then bear right at a fork onto Sophia Parkway. Continue another 2.2 miles to Green Valley Road. Cross Green Valley Road onto the paved access road for the final 0.2 mile to parking and the trailhead.

Of the many hiking trails in Folsom Lake State Recreation Area, this is one of the best: It's easy to follow, lets you access the lakeshore for a refreshing summer swim, and passes through beautiful oak woodlands far from housing developments. It's also prime habitat for spring wildflowers and a wide variety of birds that frequent the oak woodland forest, open hillsides, and blue waters of Folsom Lake.

GET MOVING

From the self-pay fee station, start uphill on the broad gravel road. The road curves left to the top of Mormon Island Dam, which keeps Folsom Lake from spilling south. Continue to the top of the northeast edge of the dam and then turn right on the dirt road just before a set of barriers. Go right and then immediately right again onto the beginning of the unsigned trail at 0.1 mile.

Climb up the main path, ignoring several smaller side trails, and soon begin contouring along an open hillside. As you continue the hike, you'll see smaller trails split off to the left and right, including several that drop down to the shore of

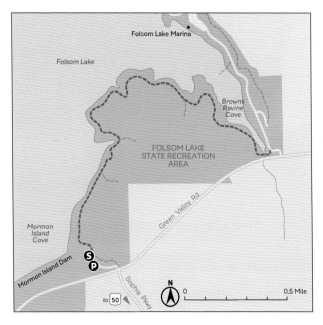

The trail to Browns Ravine passes through typical foothill vegetation.

Folsom Lake, which is frequently quite close by. There is some road noise early on, but it fades quickly.

Blue oaks, interior live oaks, and gray pines frequently provide shade along the trail. Pass a thicket of buckbrush at

0.3 mile followed quickly by several California buckeye trees, a smaller tree species that has brilliant white flowers in spring but then loses all of its leaves by late summer.

Continue along the path as it gently rises and falls, passing an assortment of wildflowers in spring and early summer. Look for *Brodiaea*, vetch, and California poppies, along with the invasive and toxic Klamath weed (St. John's wort), with its bright yellow flowers. Enjoy the floral display, but also watch for trailside poison oak, which is easy to avoid if you're paying attention.

Pass through an area of toyon, whiteleaf manzanita, coyote bush, and other chaparral species, and then, at 0.7 mile, begin arcing around the first of several coves you'll encounter on this journey. Look for willows growing below Folsom Lake's high water mark; when the lake is full, these water-loving trees are partially submerged.

Enjoy another peaceful cove at 1.2 miles before beginning a modest ascent. At 1.4 miles look for a short path on the left that goes 50 feet to the stone foundation of an old building. Back on the main trail, travel far from the water as the route passes through a peaceful oak woodland.

At 2.0 miles start descending. You'll see the extensive Folsom Lake Marina on the left across Browns Ravine Cove, with its fifteen docks mooring hundreds of boats. The path broadens to a one-lane dirt road at 2.1 miles just before a trail crossing. Go left to the adjacent lakeshore and sit by the willows; if it's midsummer or later, the blackberry bushes here will tempt you with their luscious fruit.

This lakeshore spot makes a good turnaround point, but if you want to finish the entire hike, continue on the dirt road as it contours around the large cove that shelters Folsom Lake Marina. It soon parallels heavily trafficked, quite noisy Green Valley Road and then ends beside the paved entrance to the marina at 2.4 miles. When you're ready, return the way you came.

12 Dotons Cove Trail

DISTANCE:	1.0 mile roundtrip
ELEVATION GAIN:	80 feet
HIGH POINT:	480 feet
DIFFICULTY:	Easy
FITNESS:	Walkers, hikers
FAMILY-FRIENDLY:	Yes
DOG-FRIENDLY:	On-leash
BIKE-FRIENDLY:	No
AMENITIES:	Restroom at trailhead and far end of trail
CONTACT/MAP:	Folsom Lake State Recreation Area; download map from website
GPS:	N 38°46.149', W 121°7.962'
MORE KEY INFO:	Open 6 AM to 10 PM during Daylight Saving Time, 7 AM to 7 PM rest of year; fee; first 0.2 mile wheelchair accessible

GETTING THERE

Driving: Drive I-80 about 17 miles from downtown Sacramento and take the Douglas Boulevard East exit (exit 103A). (If you're coming from the other direction, take exit 103.) Go east on Douglas Boulevard for 6.5 miles and then curve left into Folsom Lake State Recreation Area: Granite Bay. Continue on the main park road for 3.4 miles to a junction by a sign indicating Dotons Point to the right. Do not turn right; go straight for 0.1 mile to the large parking lot at Beeks Bight.

Most of the trails in Folsom Lake State Recreation Area are popular with mountain bikers, however, the Dotons Cove Trail is reserved for hikers only. It travels through peaceful oak woodlands that harbor an array of spring wildflowers, and it also takes you along a tranquil Folsom Lake cove where you can watch geese and ducks and also take a swim in warm weather. The trail features numerous signs that explain local natural and human history.

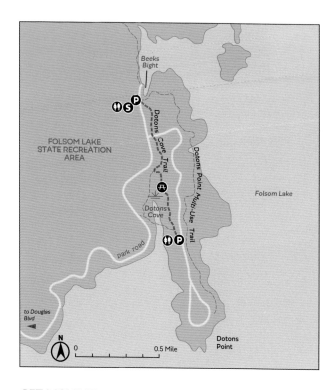

GET MOVING

The Dotons Cove Trail starts from the southwest corner of the large parking lot, on the right as you first drove in. But before you start, take a look at the lake. If it's late spring or early summer of a wet year, Folsom Lake will be nearly full; all other times it will be nearly bone-dry as you look at Beeks Bight. What's a bight, you ask? It's an Old English word for a broad bay, like the one before you. And if it's a warm day and the water level is high enough, by all means take a dip, although you'll have more swimming opportunities on the hike.

Begin at the prominent sign for Dotons Cove Trail, which is wheelchair accessible for the first 0.2 mile and open only to hikers. (The entire trail was initially constructed to be wheelchair accessible, but it needs some work.) If you look across this narrow portion of Beeks Bight, you'll spy an alternate way to return, the Dotons Point Multi-Use Trail (see Go Farther, below).

The wide and flat trail immediately crosses Beeks Bight atop a rock wall. Just beyond is the first post of the nature trail in an area of poison oak. You'll notice a lot of trailside poison oak for much of the hike, so be vigilant. The numbered posts correspond to a handout that is no longer available; however, there are a few informational signs along the route.

Walk under the shade of blue oak and interior live oak, the predominant oak species of the lower foothills of the Sierra Nevada, and be looking in the more open areas for wildflowers in spring and early summer. See the first of several benches at 0.1 mile just before passing under large gray pines, another prominent tree of the Sierra foothills.

Cross the paved road that leads to the terminus of the hike and then on to Dotons Point. Large boulders await on the far side of the road where the trail continues, and you'll then see soap plant on the right. Pass toyon shrubs to reach a buckeye tree at 0.2 mile. Unlike blue oaks, interior live oaks, and gray pines, these deciduous trees are not common, but they are quite prominent with their splays of long green leaves and showy spikes of white flowers in spring. Buckeye trees drop all their leaves in late summer, long before autumn even begins.

You'll soon see a small wetland on the right; it holds water into late spring and stays lush well into summer. Just beyond, the trail becomes too narrow for wheelchairs. Cross the wetland and then reach a bench at 0.25 mile at a trail junction. A trail goes to the right, another goes straight, and the Dotons Cove Trail, your trail, goes left. So go left and arc in front of the bench to cross the wetlands for the third and final time.

Pass a sign discussing the benefits and downsides of wildfires and then reach a bench at 0.3 mile. Look above for poison

A full Folsom Lake along the Dotons Cove Trail

oak vines that have climbed high into an interior live oak tree. Continue onward through a small grove of buckeye trees to reach two picnic tables and the first sighting of Dotons Cove. This is an excellent place to stop and take in the view; if you're lucky you'll see Canada geese or even a great blue heron.

Pass another trailside bench before reaching an open area near the lake with a sign describing Folsom Dam. Constructed between 1948 and 1956, the dam provides flood control, hydroelectric power, drinking water, and irrigation water. You now walk right beside the lake where you can take a dip or just sit among the willows and cottonwoods and enjoy the vista.

At 0.5 mile arrive at the end of the trail at a small parking lot beside the paved road that leads to Dotons Point. From here, return the way you came to the trailhead at Beeks Bight.

GO FARTHER

If you want a different route back to the trailhead, cross the paved road and look for the well-used Dotons Point Multi-Use Trail, which is also open to cyclists and equestrians. Turn left and follow it north as it runs between the paved road on the left and Folsom Lake on the right. A network of trails large and small weaves through this area, but follow the most obvious one 0.6 mile to return to the starting point of the hike.

Next page: *Blue oaks grow throughout the Sierra foothills.*

SIERRA FOOTHILLS

On clear days the high peaks of the Sierra Nevada make for a beautiful sight from the Sacramento area. This ancient and mighty mountain range slopes west toward the Central Valley, with numerous rivers carving canyons through its forested bulk.

This section focuses on trails along and near the three forks of the American River and within easy reach of Highway 49; all three forks originate as snowmelt in the High Sierra west and south of Lake Tahoe before coursing through the Sierra foothills east of Sacramento. This region contains the most scenic, wild, and physically challenging hikes in the book, although you'll definitely have company on the trails, especially in Auburn State Recreation Area.

Auburn is the anchor town in the area. The hikes begin with Hidden Falls Regional Park to the west and the Stevens Trail to the north. Then we follow Highway 49 south the rest of the way. Four trails in Auburn State Recreation Area in and near the confluence of the North Fork and Middle Fork of the American River come first, followed by three trails immediately adjacent to Highway 49, including well-known Marshall Gold Discovery State Historic Park, that all provide access to the South Fork American River.

13

Hidden Falls Regional Park

DISTANCE:	4.2 miles roundtrip
ELEVATION GAIN:	600 feet
HIGH POINT:	995 feet
DIFFICULTY:	Moderate
FITNESS:	Hikers, runners
FAMILY-FRIENDLY:	No
DOG-FRIENDLY:	On-leash
BIKE-FRIENDLY:	Yes
AMENITIES:	Restrooms at trailhead
CONTACT/MAP:	Placer County Parks and Trails; download map from website, usually available at trailhead
GPS:	N 38°57.533', W 121°09.846'
MORE KEY INFO:	Open sunrise to a half hour after sunset; parking reservations mandatory on weekends and holidays (see park website); a lot of poison oak

GETTING THERE

Driving: Pay close attention to these directions because cell service is spotty near the park. Drive about 30 miles east from downtown Sacramento on I-80 and take the Taylor Road/Highway 193 exit (exit 116). On the north side of I-80 cross Taylor Road (Highway 193) onto Ophir Road, which immediately swings to the right. After 0.3 mile on Ophir Road, turn left on Lozanos Road. After 1.0 mile on Lozanos Road, turn right on Bald Hill Road, which immediately jogs left. Continue on Bald Hill Road for 2.5 miles and then turn left onto Mount Vernon Road. After 3.7 miles on Mount Vernon Road, turn right on Mears Drive. Continue 0.5 mile on Mears Drive and then turn right onto Mears Place. Go 0.2 mile on Mears Place and then turn right for the final 0.2 mile to Hidden Falls Regional Park and the trailhead.

This not-so-hidden gem in the Sierra foothills of Placer County is popular with locals, and the reasons are obvious. Two clear and tumbling streams course through Hidden Falls Regional Park, and the steep hillsides feature oaks and pines that alternate with open areas filled with wildflowers in spring.

GET MOVING

Head to the large signboard near the restrooms to check out the poster-sized map and to grab a map to take with you. Start a gentle descent heading north on broad South Legacy Way past interior live oak, blue oak, and black oak, with open areas adorned in spring with lupine, California poppy, fairy lantern, vetch, and *Brodiaea*. The Poppy Trail, your return route, runs just below to the right.

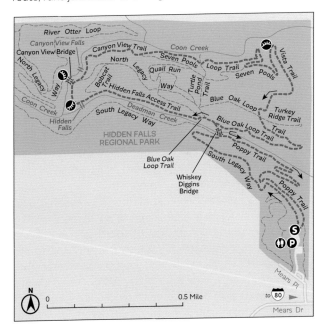

Hidden Falls, the worthy namesake of this regional park

Leave South Legacy Way as you cross Deadman Creek on the Whiskey Diggins Bridge at 0.6 mile. Walk 150 feet on North Legacy Way to a trail junction at the crossing of the Blue Oak Loop Trail. Near the end of the hike you'll return here by the right fork of the Blue Oak Loop Trail, but now go left on the Blue Oak Loop Trail for 50 feet, and then go left again onto the Hidden Falls Access Trail.

Parallel Deadman Creek downhill under oaks and past blackberries with birdsong for company. At 1.2 miles reach a trail junction with the Bobcat Trail. Go left to another trail fork at 1.3 miles, and then go left again for the brief walk to the Hidden Falls Overlook. On the way you'll see a sign explaining the geology of gold formation, with a use trail behind it dropping down to a swimming hole on Coon Creek, the larger and more prominent stream in the park. Continue to the platform and the view of impressive Hidden Falls, the park namesake, crashing down forty feet in multiple tiers. Most spectacular in winter and spring, the falls diminish markedly in summer and fall. Below Hidden Falls, Deadman Creek quickly merges into Coon Creek.

Return the way you came and hike along Coon Creek in the upstream direction to meet North Legacy Way and the Canyon View Bridge at 1.4 miles. Cross the bridge and take the short trail on the far side of the creek that climbs right to another viewing platform. Coon Creek courses below: you'll spot a small waterfall and many smooth stretches of slow water. Also gaze at the nearby hillsides, with the curved trunks and twisted branches of gray pines along their ridges.

Cross back over the Canyon View Bridge and immediately turn left on the Canyon View Trail. Head upstream to meet the Seven Pools Loop Trail at 1.7 miles. Go left and cross over the Turtle Pond Trail at 1.8 miles. (Here you can drop down to the banks of Coon Creek on the Turtle Pond Trail.) Start a substantial climb at 2.2 miles. At 2.3 miles turn left on the Seven Pools Vista Trail and continue climbing.

Look for the Seven Pools Vista on the left at 2.5 miles, just as the trail makes a sharp bend to the right. The drop-off is very steep, so watch kids and dogs carefully, and then look down on the seven beautiful pools of Coon Creek, each separated from the next by small cascades.

The climbing stops at a three-way trail junction at 2.9 miles. Here the Seven Pools Vista Trail ends, the Turkey Ridge Trail goes left, and the Blue Oak Loop Trail goes to the right and straight. Follow the Blue Oak Loop Trail straight and downhill. The path is well-named; it travels through open blue oak woodlands, a great place to hear and see acorn woodpeckers.

Reach the main junction of trails from near the beginning of the hike at 3.5 miles, just 150 feet from the bridge across Deadman Creek. Go left on North Legacy Way to the previously encountered bridge across Deadman Creek. South Legacy Way rises up to the right back to the trailhead. You can take South Legacy Way or go left on the Poppy Trail, which initially runs upstream near Deadman Creek before switch-backing up to the parking lot at 4.2 miles.

GO FARTHER

If you have the park map, you can explore the many other trails that intersect those described here. All trail junctions are clearly signed.

14 Stevens Trail

DISTANCE:	7.0 miles roundtrip
ELEVATION GAIN:	1400 feet
HIGH POINT:	2400 feet
DIFFICULTY:	Challenging
FITNESS:	Hikers, runners
FAMILY-FRIENDLY:	No
DOG-FRIENDLY:	On-leash
BIKE-FRIENDLY:	No
AMENITIES:	Restroom at trailhead
CONTACT/MAP:	Bureau of Land Management, Mother Lode Field Office; no map online
GPS:	N 39°06.322', W 120°56.844'
MORE KEY INFO:	Open daily year-round; bring a lot of water; return is uphill and often exposed; a lot of poison oak

GETTING THERE

Driving: Drive I-80 to Colfax and take exit 135 (signed for Colfax and Grass Valley). Reach the east side of the freeway (opposite side of freeway from the main part of Colfax) and turn left on North Canyon Way. Drive north beside the freeway 0.6 mile to a parking lot on the left where the trail begins.

This hike packs in all the best of the lower Sierra Nevada. You'll travel a path rich in human history, wander through

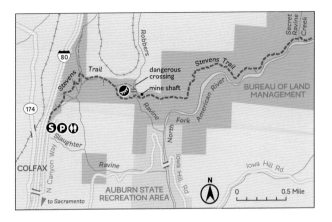

shady forests, visit a tumbling waterfall, and view the North Fork American River from high above and streamside.

GET MOVING

The broad trail begins on the east side of the parking lot. The entire route is the historic Stevens Trail. Soon after arriving in the area in 1859, Truman Allen Stevens built the route, connecting Colfax with the booming mining area of Iowa Hill on the opposite side of the North Fork American River. He charged miners and others to cross the American River on a self-propelled cable car.

Descend gently and soon cross the first of four small streams you'll encounter over the first 0.7 mile as the sound of the freeway fades away. The route is shaded first by California laurel and big-leaf maple, later by extensive stands of canyon live oak. Immediately after crossing the fourth and largest creek, turn right on the dirt road, as indicated by a trail sign.

Encounter ample spring wildflowers in the more open environment. The dirt road begins an ascent at 0.8 mile to reach a saddle at 1.0 mile. Cross the saddle, ignoring the dirt road that rises steeply to the right, and walk through a forest

Downstream view of the North Fork American River from the Stevens Trail

that includes gray pine, Douglas fir, and the occasional ponderosa pine.

Descend to a trail fork at 1.3 miles. A sign indicates that the bike trail goes right and the hiker-only trail goes left. The two rejoin about 0.4 mile farther on the far side of Robbers Ravine waterfall. Your main route is the bicycle trail because it's far safer. Doing the entire portion of the hiker trail involves crossing the Robbers Ravine stream immediately above a twenty-foot portion of the waterfall. This crossing can be quite dangerous because the wet rocks are slippery and the consequences of a fall disastrous. However, you should definitely hike 0.2 mile on the hiker trail to a point just before the dangerous crossing to get the best view of the multiple tiers of the waterfall tumbling 300 feet or more through the narrow defile; also take the nearby forty-foot side path through brush to an open expanse of rock for a broad view of the North Fork American River canyon, the waterfall, and the impressive rock retaining wall high above built for the railroad tracks.

Back on the bicycle portion of the trail, continue the descent. A hundred yards beyond the trail fork stay left on the main path as a dirt road branches right. At 1.5 miles cross Robbers Ravine at the lower portion of the waterfall, a cool, shady spot that invites you to linger.

Shortly beyond the creek the hiker portion of the trail drops in from the left. Continue through an open area where some of the metamorphic rock that predominates in this region has tumbled down from cliffs above to create a talus slope. You'll see a mine shaft on the left at 1.7 miles (stay out), and you'll see more evidence of mining farther along the trail.

The path then narrows and runs along the cliffside with steep drop-offs to the right. Pause here to take in the wild beauty of the North Fork American River canyon. Rocky, tree-clad slopes plunge abruptly to the tumbling green water that cascades downstream. The North Fork American River crosses under the Iowa Hill Road bridge and then disappears westerly on its journey to meet the Sacramento River.

Views of ravine and river continue as the route progresses downhill in the upstream direction. At 2.8 miles the first of several side paths drops steeply to the river. Continue on the main route to reach alder-shaded Secret Ravine Creek at 3.5 miles. The trail and the hike end on the far side at a flat beside the North Fork American River, where you'll see ample evidence that this was the crossing site for the Stevens Trail. If it's a hot day and you're a good swimmer, carefully make your way down to a large swimming hole just downstream of the confluence of the river and Secret Ravine Creek. When you're rested and ready, make the climb back to the trailhead.

15 Mountain Quarries Railroad Trail

DISTANCE:	3.4 miles roundtrip
ELEVATION GAIN:	350 feet
HIGH POINT:	780 feet
DIFFICULTY:	Easy to moderate
FITNESS:	Walkers, runners
FAMILY-FRIENDLY:	Yes
DOG-FRIENDLY:	On-leash
BIKE-FRIENDLY:	No
AMENITIES:	Restroom on east side of Mountain Quarries Railroad Bridge
CONTACT/MAP:	Auburn State Recreation Area; download map from website
GPS:	N 38°54.899', W 121°2.392'
MORE KEY INFO:	Open 7 AM to sunset; free parking and entrance at this location at time of writing

GETTING THERE

Driving: Drive I-80 about 33 miles from downtown Sacramento to Auburn. Take the Highway 49 South exit (exit 119C for Elm Avenue). Drive 0.2 mile east on Elm Avenue and then turn left onto Highway 49 toward Placerville. Continue south and downhill on Highway 49 to its junction with Old Foresthill Road near the confluence of the North Fork and Middle Fork of the American River, 2.5 miles from I-80. Turn right to stay on Highway 49, cross the bridge, and then park on the right side of the road just beyond.

The beautiful North Fork American River is the highlight of this easy walk along the old Mountain Quarries Railroad bed. You'll always hear the river, you'll frequently see it, and several side paths take you down to its banks.

GET MOVING

Walk Highway 49 back toward the North Fork American River to find the beginning of the trail on the left side just before the bridge. The route passes gray pines, interior live oaks, toyon and manzanita bushes, and a bit of poison oak.

Reach the Mountain Quarries Railroad Bridge at 0.1 mile. You'll see a trail heading left and uphill (see Trail 16, Pointed Rocks), and a buckeye tree in bush form on the right. Make your way onto the historic bridge, built in 1912; at one time the railroad used the bridge to transport limestone from a nearby quarry to Auburn. It's known locally as the "No Hands Bridge" because, before the railings were installed, horse riders would cross without holding the reins while yelling, "Look, no hands!"

Pause on the bridge and look just below to see the coursing water of the North Fork American River, hemmed in by steep slopes stretching high above. In the upstream direction you'll see the Highway 49 bridge nearby, with the Foresthill Bridge both farther away and much higher. You'll likely also see numerous cliff swallows darting about.

Reach the far side of the bridge and read about the bridge's history before turning left. You're on the Western States Trail, which once stretched from Utah to Sacramento and is now famous for endurance runs and horse rides. As you move farther through the canyon in the downstream direction, the sound of the river and increasing distance muffle most noise from Highway 49.

At 0.3 mile look for an obvious, steep trail that drops 200 yards to the bank of the river, where you can now experience the North Fork up close. If it's a warm day and you're a good swimmer, you can also take a dip in the area where the current slows. Smaller paths drop down to the river as you continue the hike.

At 0.5 mile the path passes under the shade of black oaks and interior live oaks, and views of the river are scarce for a while. At 0.7 mile leave the railroad bed for the first time near the first of several concrete abutments that served as supports for a long-gone railroad bridge and briefly descend a small gully before climbing to rejoin the bed of the railroad.

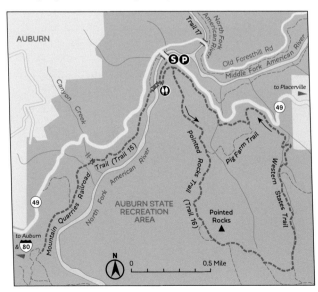

The Mountain Quarries Railroad Bridge spans the North Fork American River.

A deeper gully awaits at 1.0 mile, this time to cross Canyon Creek on a wooden bridge just below pretty little Canyon Creek Falls. Horseback riders have termed this stream crossing the "Black Hole of Calcutta." Go left at a fork at 1.3 miles (a trail to the right climbs steeply for 0.4 mile to the Auburn State Recreation Area Headquarters on Highway 49), staying on the gentle grade of the old railroad bed. Pass under a large rock outcrop at 1.5 miles and continue to a trail fork with the Riverview Trail at 1.7 miles, the turnaround point for this hike.

GO FARTHER

Continue farther on the Riverview Trail, or do all or part of the Pointed Rocks Trail (Trail 16), which leaves this hike on the east side of the Mountain Quarries Railroad Bridge.

16   Pointed Rocks

DISTANCE:	4.6 miles roundtrip
ELEVATION GAIN:	1100 feet
HIGH POINT:	1640 feet
DIFFICULTY:	Moderate to challenging
FITNESS:	Hikers, runners
FAMILY-FRIENDLY:	No
DOG-FRIENDLY:	On-leash
BIKE-FRIENDLY:	No
AMENITIES:	Restrooms on east side of Mountain Quarries Railroad Bridge
CONTACT/MAP:	Auburn State Recreation Area; download map from website
GPS:	N 38°54.899', W 121°2.392'
MORE KEY INFO:	Open 7 AM to sunset; free parking and entrance at this location at time of writing

GETTING THERE

Driving: Drive I-80 about 33 miles from downtown Sacramento to Auburn. Take the Highway 49 South exit (exit 119C for Elm Avenue). Drive 0.2 mile east on Elm Avenue and then turn left onto Highway 49 toward Placerville. Continue south and downhill on Highway 49 to its junction with Old Foresthill Road near the confluence of the North Fork and Middle Fork of the American River, 2.5 miles from I-80. Turn right to stay on Highway 49, cross the bridge, and then park on the right side of the road just beyond.

This hike is one of the most spectacular in Auburn State Recreation Area, but you'll have to work a bit to complete it. You'll climb nearly 1000 feet up Training Hill to win the reward of sweeping views of valley, hill, and mountain from Pointed Rocks. Try it in spring for the bonus reward of wildflowers on the open slopes.

GET MOVING

Head back toward the Highway 49 bridge to find the trailhead. Start on a dirt road that offers an excellent view of the North Fork American River down below to the right.

Arrive at the Mountain Quarries Railroad Bridge at 0.1 mile. Your route goes left up the single-track trail, but for now take a short stroll onto the bridge (see Trail 15). Here you'll see wooded hillsides dropping steeply down to the North Fork American River, with the Highway 49 bridge and the Foresthill Bridge in the upstream direction.

Back on the east side of the bridge, take the narrow trail, here the combined Western States Trail and Pointed Rocks Trail, which is signed for the town of Cool. Climb briefly and then continue north on level trail to a fork at 0.3 mile. The Western States Trail, your return route, goes left.

The beginning of the Pointed Rocks Trail: time to climb!

You, however, turn right and begin a long and steep southerly climb on the Pointed Rocks Trail for the next 1.1 miles, the
tread a wide and eroding service road, gaining nearly 1000
feet of elevation in the process. Pass through an open forest of typical Sierra foothill trees, including ponderosa pine,
knobcone pine, gray pine, interior live oak, blue oak, and a few
Douglas fir, and pause occasionally to look down on the North
Fork American River.

At 0.9 mile, about halfway through the ascent, the Pig
Farm Trail comes in from the left. Stay right and keep climbing, unless you want a much shorter hike. (The Pig Farm Trail
cuts east to the Western States Trail, the return route.) As you
puff your way through this tough stretch, you'll understand
why this route is also called the Training Hill Trail.

You'll be grateful to arrive at the ridge at 1.4 miles. A rolling
open blue-oak woodland with coffeeberry and toyon spreads
before you as you walk the wide path, enjoying westward views
of foothills sloping down to the Sacramento Valley. Reach a
trail fork at 1.6 miles. Go left and soon arrive at Pointed Rocks,
an array of relatively large limestone boulders encrusted
with lichens. This is a good spot to gaze east at the forested
mountains rising to the High Sierra and a good turnaround
point if you want a shorter hike.

To continue, return to the main path and contour along
the open hillside beyond Pointed Rocks, staying left at a fork
with an unnamed trail, to reach the Olmstead Loop Trail at 1.8
miles. Go left and follow the Olmstead Loop Trail for 0.3 mile,
and then turn left at the next junction, signed for the William
T. Robie Trail.

Go 0.2 mile and then turn left at 2.3 miles onto the Western States Trail (also called the William T. Robie Trail). This
route, known for its hundred-mile endurance runs and horse
rides, stays on the ridge awhile before dropping into a more
shaded canyon. Go left at 2.9 miles at the junction with the
Short-Cut Trail, staying on the Western States Trail. Begin

walking within sight and sound of Highway 49 at 3.3 miles. At 3.6 miles you encounter the eastern end of the Pig Farm Trail. Stay right and descend gently on the Western States Trail to the meeting with the Pointed Rocks Trail at 4.3 miles (where you began the climb up Training Hill). From here, turn right for the final 0.3 mile back to the trailhead on previously hiked trail and past the Mountain Quarries Railroad Bridge.

GO FARTHER
The Mountain Quarries Railroad Trail (Trail 15) is the best bet. You'll appreciate the mostly level path.

17 Lake Clementine Trail

DISTANCE:	4.6 miles roundtrip
ELEVATION GAIN:	750 feet
HIGH POINT:	955 feet
DIFFICULTY:	Moderate
FITNESS:	Hikers, runners
FAMILY-FRIENDLY:	Yes
DOG-FRIENDLY:	On-leash
BIKE-FRIENDLY:	Yes
AMENITIES:	Restrooms at trailhead
CONTACT/MAP:	Auburn State Recreation Area; download map from website
GPS:	N 38°54.934', W 121°2.151'
MORE KEY INFO:	Open 7 AM to sunset; parking fee (pay at trailhead); swimming opportunities; popular with mountain bikers

GETTING THERE
Driving: Drive I-80 about 33 miles from downtown Sacramento to Auburn. Take the Highway 49 South exit (exit 119C for Elm Avenue). Drive 0.2 mile east on Elm Avenue and then turn left onto Highway 49 toward Placerville. Continue south and downhill on Highway 49 a total of 2.5 miles from I-80 and

continue straight onto Old Foresthill Road. Continue another 0.4 mile and park in the lot on the right, just past the bridge over the North Fork American River and near the confluence with the Middle Fork.

The Lake Clementine Trail is popular year-round, and for good reason. In summer hikers can take a dip at Clarks Hole, and spring brings impressive wildflower blooms. Every season features the imposing scenery of steep slopes dropping down to the North Fork American River and the impressive visage of massive sheets of water spilling over the North Fork Dam at Lake Clementine.

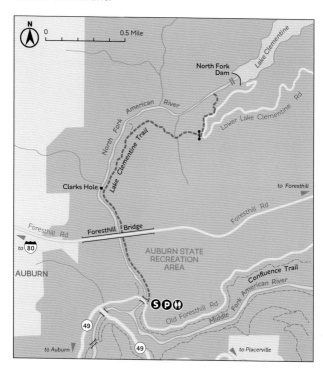

GET MOVING

Cross Old Foresthill Road and walk to the near side of the bridge to find the Lake Clementine Trail. The route begins as a dirt road, and the scenery is stunning. The North Fork American River rushes just below, with steep slopes rising nearly 1000 feet on both sides. The impressive Foresthill Bridge is high above and directly ahead in the upstream direction. Be sure to turn around and look in the downstream direction at the confluence of the North and Middle Forks of the American River.

Walk through open woodlands populated by gray pine and interior live oak, as well as lupines, vetch, California poppies, and a wide array of other wildflowers in spring. Stay left at 0.1 mile when a trail rises uphill to the right, and then stop near a picnic table at 0.2 mile to admire nearby cottonwood trees and blue oaks and to look across the river at concrete abutments, the only remnants of an old bridge.

Pass under the imposing Foresthill Bridge at 0.5 mile. At 730 feet above the North Fork American River, it's the highest bridge in California and the fourth highest in the United States. It was completed in 1973 to span the proposed Auburn Reservoir. The Auburn Dam (Auburn Reservoir) project was abandoned in the 1980s for a variety of reasons, including potential earthquake risk and environmental concerns.

As you continue, look for a broad, slow part of the river: Clarks Hole. Take the short side path on the left at 0.7 mile that quickly brings you down to the sandy beach. Clarks Hole is a popular summer swimming spot for locals. The water is relatively warm here because it comes from the top of Lake Clementine, where it absorbs heat from the sun.

Farther along the main trail, look for more remnants of old bridges and then begin a long climb of moderate gradient along the canyon slope. Look for canyon live oaks, plus common chaparral species like toyon and whiteleaf manzanita.

At a height of 730 feet, the Foresthill Bridge is the tallest in California.

As you continue, you'll likely hear the roar of the water tumbling from Lake Clementine over North Fork Dam.

The dirt path and the climbing end at 1.9 miles at a gate on paved Lower Lake Clementine Road. Turn left on the road, descend 0.3 mile, and then look for an unmarked path on the left. Descend gently 0.1 mile to an overlook point near North Fork Dam. Now the artificial waterfall comes into full glory, with flows highest in winter and spring. You'll also see the surface of Lake Clementine and, if it's summer, a lot of boats.

Look for a single-track trail that drops down the river just below North Fork Dam. Here you'll find another spectacular view of the waterfall plus access to a deep swimming hole. When you're ready, return the way you came.

GO FARTHER
From the parking area, walk down to the banks of the Middle Fork American River and take the Confluence Trail upstream.

18 Foresthill Divide Loop Trail

DISTANCE:	9.2-mile loop
ELEVATION GAIN:	1500 feet
HIGH POINT:	1930 feet
DIFFICULTY:	Moderate to challenging
FITNESS:	Hikers, runners
FAMILY-FRIENDLY:	Yes
DOG-FRIENDLY:	On-leash
BIKE-FRIENDLY:	Yes
AMENITIES:	Restrooms at trailhead
CONTACT/MAP:	Auburn State Recreation Area; download map from website
GPS:	N 38°56.556', W 120°58.954'
MORE KEY INFO:	Open 7 AM to sunset; parking fee (pay at trailhead); poison oak; watch for cyclists

GETTING THERE
Driving: Drive I-80 about 35 miles from downtown Sacramento to Auburn. Take the Foresthill Road exit (exit 121). Go right on Foresthill Road and drive 4.6 miles east/northeast and then park in the large lot on the right. If you want to arrange a shuttle, park the second car another 3.6 miles farther at the large parking lot for the eastern trailhead on the left (4.5 miles into the hiking, running, and biking route).

The Foresthill Divide Loop Trail runs through oak woodlands, chaparral, and pine forest as it travels along first the south side then the north side of Foresthill Divide, the ridge separating the Middle Fork American River from the North Fork American River. You'll get excellent views of both forks (especially the Middle Fork), along with expansive views of hills, ridges, and mountains. The first half of the loop along the Middle Fork side of the divide has the best views.

GET MOVING

Head over to the green gate to find the start of the trail, with a large signboard just beyond that has a map of the area.

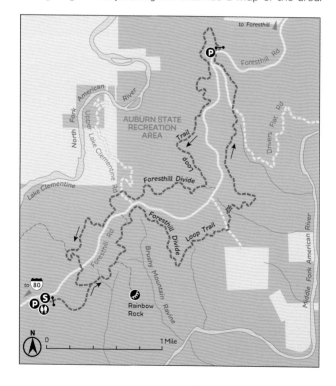

Curve left and walk under the shade of interior live oaks and blue oaks to soon enter an open meadow dotted with even more beautiful blue oaks. Walk through more open areas filled with wildflowers in spring months: look for lupine, California poppy, vetch, *Brodiaea*, and others. You'll also see whiteleaf manzanita, toyon, buckbrush, chamise, and other typical chaparral plants.

Reach a trail fork at 0.5 mile, the start of the loop portion of the Foresthill Divide Loop Trail. You'll eventually return via the left fork, but for now turn right and begin the counterclockwise circumambulation. Leave the open meadow and road noise behind as you descend through shady oak forest.

At 0.6 mile the vegetation opens up to give a good southerly view of the Middle Fork American River drainage. At 1.0 mile an unmarked side path on the right makes an interesting addition to the hike: the trail runs 0.4 mile through chaparral and gray pine to Rainbow Rock and an overlook of the Middle Fork American River, with a full southerly vista. Back on the main loop trail, continue left another 0.4 mile to meet a dirt road at 1.4 miles near Foresthill Road; go right to stay on the trail.

The path narrows (watch for poison oak) as it continues through open oak forest. Excellent views await at 2.3 miles, with a broad southerly vista of the Middle Fork drainage and a westward view that includes ridges and valleys, along with the limestone quarry near the town of Cool. At 3.1 miles bear left at an unsigned trail junction and then quickly right at another unsigned junction, and then cross a creek on a wooden bridge at 3.3 miles.

The path continues to gently rise and fall, and then meets dirt Drivers Flat Road at 4.0 miles. You can either walk on Drivers Flat Road or stay on the actual trail that borders the road on the right; either way, reach Foresthill Road at 4.4 miles. If you like open oak woodlands and more frequent vistas, return to the trailhead the way you came.

The Foresthill Divide Loop Trail runs through beautiful oak woodlands.

If you want to complete the mostly forested second half of the Foresthill Divide Loop Trail, carefully cross Foresthill Road and then continue to the right to reach the eastern trailhead for the Foresthill Divide Loop Trail at 4.5 miles. You'll find parking and the trailhead on the left side of Foresthill Road (where you've left a second vehicle if doing a shuttle).

Head to the back of the parking lot to find the continuation of the trail at a gate. The path quickly passes through a saddle to the North Fork American River side of the Foresthill Divide. You now travel through a mixed pine and oak forest. Views are less frequent than on the Middle Fork side, but you'll still catch glimpses of the North Fork American River and Lake Clementine.

Stay right at a trail fork at 5.9 miles, and then cross dirt Upper Lake Clementine Road at 7.0 miles. Continue another 1.1 miles through oak and madrone woodlands to a trail fork at 8.1 miles. Turn left at the fork and go 0.3 mile to carefully cross Foresthill Road. Continue another 0.3 mile to finally close the Foresthill Divide Trail Loop at 8.7 miles. Turn right to walk the half mile back to the trailhead on the trail you started on.

19 Cronan Ranch Regional Trails Park

DISTANCE:	4.1-mile loop
ELEVATION GAIN:	500 feet
HIGH POINT:	1050 feet
DIFFICULTY:	Moderate
FITNESS:	Hikers, runners
FAMILY-FRIENDLY:	Yes
DOG-FRIENDLY:	Yes, as long as under full command of owners; grazing sheep
BIKE-FRIENDLY:	Yes
AMENITIES:	Restrooms at trailhead and along South Fork American River; picnic tables along river
CONTACT/MAP:	Bureau of Land Management, Mother Lode Field Office; map online and at trailhead
GPS:	N 38°49.632', W 120°59.339'
MORE KEY INFO:	Open daily year-round

GETTING THERE

Driving: Drive I-80 about 33 miles from downtown Sacramento to Auburn. Take the Highway 49 South exit (exit 119C for Elm Avenue). Drive 0.2 mile east on Elm Avenue and then turn left onto Highway 49 toward Placerville. Continue south and east a total of 11.3 miles from I-80 and then turn right on dirt Pedro Hill Road. (From the junction of Highway 49 and US Highway 50 in Placerville, Pedro Hill Road is 14.7 miles northwest on Highway 49.) You'll then see the large trailhead parking lot on the left.

This hike highlights the best of the Sierra Nevada foothills. The former ranch features broad oak-dotted grasslands that blaze with wildflowers in spring, and the trail system accesses the banks of the South Fork American River where you can swim, fish, and picnic. Plus, the entire trail is on dirt roads wide enough for you to walk side by side with your companions.

GET MOVING

Climb gently south on broad dirt and gravel Cronan Ranch Road for 0.2 mile to a signboard on the left at a fork in the trail. Take a good look to familiarize yourself with the trail system. You'll eventually return to this spot via Cronan Ranch Road, but now the real journey begins with a left on the Down and Up Trail, a single-lane dirt road.

The true beauty of this special part of the Sierra foothills now unfolds. Ridges topped by gray pine give way to the broad curves of grassland slopes with scattered interior live oak and blue oak. In spring swaths of wildflowers clothe the slopes in blue and yellow, and year-round you'll hear meadowlark song and spy hawks and vultures circling high above.

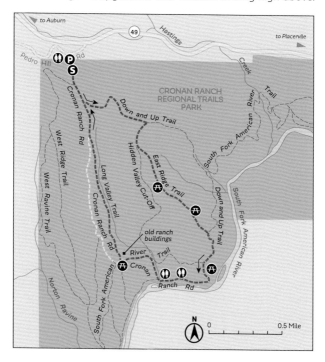

The entire drainage feeds south to the South Fork American River, the main destination of this hike.

At 0.8 mile leave the Down and Up Trail to go right on the Hidden Valley Cut-Off Trail (the sign may be hidden in tall grass), the highest point of the hike. At 1.0 mile leave the Hidden Valley Cut-Off Trail at an unsigned junction to go left on the East Ridge Trail and start a long and gentle descent toward the unseen South Fork American River. Stop at the picnic table on the right at 1.1 miles to sit under the shade of a large blue oak and take in the broad panorama of hill and valley, which now includes a sliver of the river below.

Meet the Down and Up Trail again at 1.8 miles; here it is also part of the South Fork American River Trail. Join the combined trail by going right, where you'll pass through a fence and then descend to another fork at 2.0 miles, this time with Cronan Ranch Road. Go left on Cronan Ranch Road and descend toward the sound of the river.

You soon reach the South Fork American River, which begins as snowmelt in the High Sierra just south of Lake Tahoe and ends at Folsom Lake. Here it flows clear and cool, bordered on this side by willows, cottonwoods, oaks, and Oregon ash, with some ponderosa pines on the far side. Strong and experienced swimmers will find spots to take a dip beside the bank, and everyone will enjoy relaxing at the several picnic tables and watching the river flow. For your convenience, three sets of pit toilets line the section of the trail that parallels the river.

Walk downstream near the river for the next several hundred yards to cross the stream draining the main valley at 2.4 miles, here shaded by black walnut trees, beside the last set of toilets and a trail fork. Go right to stay on graveled Cronan Ranch Road and, always staying on the gravel road and ignoring all trail junctions, begin a long climb that won't end until you're nearly back at the trailhead. Stay left on Cronan Ranch Road at a meeting with the South Fork American River

Sheep graze in Cronan Ranch Regional Trails Park.

Trail at 2.6 miles, which is the same as Cronan Ranch Road for the next 0.2 mile.

Arrive at old ranch buildings at 2.8 miles. Visitors are not allowed to enter the buildings, but you can sit at the picnic table under the spreading branches of a massive blue oak tree if you want a rest. Just beyond the ranch buildings is a three-way trail junction. To the left is the South Fork American River Trail. Straight ahead is Cronan Ranch Road, and to the right is the Long Valley Trail.

Take the Long Valley Trail and continue uphill and north through the broad, beautiful valley. The stream runs from winter into late spring, and its waters support cattails and willows, with a vast array of wildflowers growing near the stream and throughout the grasslands on both sides. Meet Cronan Ranch Road at 3.7 miles and go right for 0.2 mile to the signboard with the trail map you encountered near the beginning of the journey. Continue straight and downhill for the final 0.2 mile to the trailhead.

GO FARTHER

Many other trails in Cronan Ranch Regional Trails Park are worthy of exploration. Consider exploring these three more extensively: the Down and Up, South Fork American River, and West Ridge Trails.

20 Dave Moore Nature Area

DISTANCE:	1.2-mile loop
ELEVATION GAIN:	50 feet
HIGH POINT:	750 feet
DIFFICULTY:	Easy
FITNESS:	Walkers, hikers
FAMILY-FRIENDLY:	Yes
DOG-FRIENDLY:	On-leash
BIKE-FRIENDLY:	No
AMENITIES:	Restroom at trailhead; trailside picnic table
CONTACT/MAP:	Bureau of Land Management, Mother Lode Field Office; map online and at trailhead
GPS:	N 38˚48.852', W 120˚55.326'
MORE KEY INFO:	Open daily year-round; wheelchair accessible for first 0.4 mile

GETTING THERE

Driving: Drive I-80 about 33 miles from downtown Sacramento to Auburn. Take the Highway 49 South exit (exit 119C for Elm Avenue). Drive 0.2 mile east on Elm Avenue and then turn left onto Highway 49 toward Placerville. Continue south and east a total of 15.4 miles from I-80 and then turn right on a dirt road on the south side of Highway 49; the dirt road runs between a beckoning set of rock walls, with the right side marked by a "Dave Moore Nature Area" sign. The dirt road dead-ends at a spacious parking lot. If you approach from Placerville, this access road is 10.6 miles northwest of the

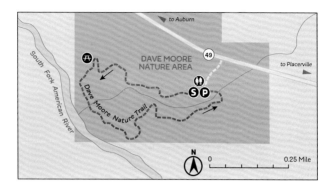

junction of Highway 49 and US Highway 50 in Placerville and 0.1 mile west of Deloro Lane.

This easy loop trail through the Dave Moore Nature Area offers a lot of natural beauty for very little effort. It travels through typical Sierra foothill vegetation on the way to the banks of the South Fork American River, where strong swimmers can immerse themselves on hot days. The level path is especially attractive for families who use strollers, people in wheelchairs, and anyone wanting a quick hike with easy access from Highway 49.

GET MOVING

The loop trail begins at the far end of the parking area most distant from Highway 49 and beside a large kiosk with a map and other information. Immediately reach a memorial plaque dedicated to Dave Moore. Dave was a range conservationist with the Bureau of Land Management who was stricken with multiple sclerosis at age thirty-five and eventually passed away. His coworkers built this path, the first 0.4 mile wheelchair accessible, in his honor.

Cross the first of eight wooden bridges that span small seasonal creeks along the route. Walk under the shade of

Oaks border much of the Dave Moore Nature Trail.

evergreen interior live oaks and past an understory of buck-brush, blackberries, and poison oak. Look above the oaks to spot a few gray pines and ponderosa pines.

Cross a second wooden bridge at 0.1 mile and enjoy trailside lupine blossoms in spring. The path soon traverses a lush ravine rampant with willows and blackberries before crossing a third bridge.

Encounter a grove of madrone trees at 0.2 mile, where you'll spot an intriguing mushroom-shaped rock on the right that's several feet high. This is a good spot to let kids explore before moving on.

You'll soon encounter a trailside picnic table under the ample shade of ponderosa pine and interior live oak; wander next through a stately grove of ponderosa pine. Look on the right side of the path for a rock wall built by Chinese laborers during the gold rush era in the mid-nineteenth century, and then cross the fourth wooden bridge at 0.3 mile. You'll see more historical rock wall remnants on the left at 0.4 mile as the sound of the river fills your ears.

The trail is washed out a bit at 0.4 mile where it crosses two more bridges; this is the end of the wheelchair-accessible portion of the path. Just beyond these two bridges the route arrives at the highlight of the hike: the banks of the South Fork American River, bordered by willows and Oregon ash trees. Sit awhile and watch the river flow and look for blue herons. If it's a warm day and you're a good swimmer with experience in rapidly moving streams enjoy a swim.

When you're ready, continue on the trail, crossing the seventh wooden bridge at 0.5 mile. Walk through an area of willows and cottonwoods, with the sound of the river to the right. Look for side paths that lead to the riverbanks.

Walk among large boulders through oak woodlands dominated by interior live oak and buckbrush. At 0.7 mile the trail curves left and away from the river and rises gently. This is the best part of the hike to see a variety of spring wildflowers. Pass through a grove of blue oaks at 1.1 miles, and then cross one last wooden bridge before arriving at the opposite side of the parking lot from where you started.

21 Marshall Gold Discovery State Historic Park

DISTANCE:	3.3-mile loop
ELEVATION GAIN:	750 feet
HIGH POINT:	1260 feet
DIFFICULTY:	Moderate
FITNESS:	Walkers, hikers, runners
FAMILY-FRIENDLY:	Yes, a lot to interest kids
DOG-FRIENDLY:	On-leash
BIKE-FRIENDLY:	No
AMENITIES:	Restrooms in developed areas, picnic tables, water fountains, museum, store
CONTACT/MAP:	Marshall Gold Discovery State Historic Park; download map from website; combination map and brochure available at park
GPS:	N 38°48.302', W 120°53.699'
MORE KEY INFO:	Open daily 8 AM to 5 PM (later in summer), except Thanksgiving and Christmas; museum open 9 AM to 4 PM, except Thanksgiving and Christmas; fee

GETTING THERE

Driving: Drive I-80 about 33 miles from downtown Sacramento to Auburn. Take the Highway 49 South exit (exit 119C for Elm Avenue). Drive 0.2 mile east on Elm Avenue and then turn left onto Highway 49 toward Placerville. Continue south and east a total of 17.7 miles from I-80 to Marshall Gold Discovery State Historic Park. (From Placerville, the park is 8.3 miles northwest of the junction of Highway 49 and US Highway 50 in Placerville.) Pull into the northernmost parking lot on the east side (North Beach), the first lot on the left if you're coming from Auburn.

This hike in Marshall Gold Discovery State Historic Park lets you explore the natural and human history of this area, the latter having defined a crucial era in the development of

California. Before you start moving, take a few minutes to appreciate the historical significance of this park, from its days when native Miwok and Nisenan peoples populated the area to the original Gold Discovery Site. Many buildings and other relics from the gold mining days still survive here, and

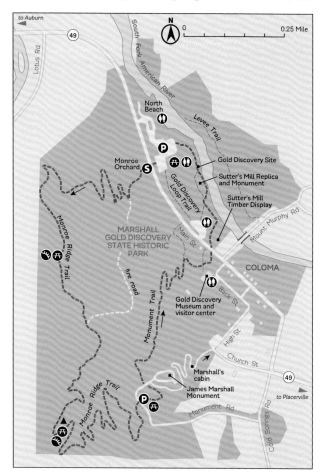

The park features many relics of the California gold rush days.

you'll have ample opportunity to visit them after exploring the natural areas of Monroe Ridge on the park's western boundary (see "The California Gold Rush" sidebar).

GET MOVING

To begin the hike, head to the southern part of the parking lot and carefully cross Highway 49 at the fence gap, following the sign for the Monroe Ridge Trail. The route starts in Monroe Orchard. The Monroe family came to California as slaves; they were freed when California joined the United States, and they eventually owned substantial portions of the land that makes up the park.

At 0.1 mile the Monroe Ridge Trail meets an old dirt fire road. Go right and begin a significant climb via well-graded

THE CALIFORNIA GOLD RUSH

On January 24, 1848, James W. Marshall, a partner in a lumber venture in Coloma on the South Fork American River, discovered gold in a tailrace constructed for Sutter's Mill. News of the discovery soon leaked and the California gold rush was on.

Over the next several years, three hundred thousand people came to California to seek their fortunes by mining the precious metal in Northern California and the Sierra foothills, including along the South, Middle, and North Forks of the American River and their tributaries. In response to the influx of miners, the city of Sacramento was laid out in 1848 and incorporated in 1849. The economic boom and the swelling population propelled California to statehood in 1850, and numerous mining towns sprang up east of Sacramento, including Auburn and Placerville.

The gold rush, however, came at a steep price. Native Californians suffered immensely at the hands of the newcomers: disease, starvation, and murder led to sharp declines in population. The environment also suffered: miners leveled forests, dammed and diverted streams, and demolished whole hillsides through hydraulic mining.

Signs of the gold rush are evident throughout the Sierra foothills, including along and near the hiking trails in Auburn State Recreation Area and along Highway 49.

switchbacks through a forest of interior live oak, gray pine, and ponderosa pine, with a substantial understory of manzanita and other chaparral plants, including poison oak.

The trail turns south at 0.6 mile and begins traveling on and near the crest of Monroe Ridge. Reach a high spot at 0.9 mile that features a picnic table and an excellent view of the entire park spread below to the east. At 1.1 miles the dirt fire road encountered early in the hike comes up from the left; stay right along Monroe Ridge.

The highest point arrives at 1.6 miles, along with another picnic table and scenic views. From here, the path switchbacks downhill and easterly through open areas flush with wild-flowers in spring to end at a picnic area parking lot near the James Marshall Monument at 2.2 miles. Turn left on paved Monument Road and continue 0.1 mile to the James Marshall Monument, erected in 1890. The large statue of James Marshall points to the area where he discovered gold. Take his direction and head that way.

From the base of the steps leading to the monument, head to the nearby park employee residence to find the sign for the Monument Trail. Descend north 0.6 mile on the broad path to its end among historical buildings along Highway 49. The Gold Discovery Museum and visitor center are just to the right, and are well worth the time. You can also explore other historical buildings near Highway 49.

For the final part of the hike, carefully cross Highway 49 just left (north) of Mount Murphy Road. Pick up the Gold Discovery Loop Trail near the Sutter's Mill Timber Display and walk north near the west bank of the South Fork American River past the Sutter's Mill Replica and Monument and the Gold Discovery Site to reach your vehicle at 3.3 miles.

GO FARTHER

Use the detailed map in the park brochure to guide you to the many historical sites, and don't forget to visit the excellent museum. There's also the 0.4-mile-long Levee Trail on the far side of the South Fork American River, reached via Mount Murphy Road.

Next page: *The Mokelumne River along the Lodi Lake Nature Trail (Trail 25)*

SOUTH OF SACRAMENTO

The rich agricultural land of the Sacramento–San Joaquin River Delta region is cut by Interstate 5 and Highway 99 running south from Sacramento. Here multiple rivers converge, from the mighty Sacramento and San Joaquin Rivers from the north and south respectively, to the Cosumnes and Mokelumne Rivers, which rush west from the High Sierra.

This area lies smack in the middle of the controversy about how to divide a supply of California water that's inadequate to meet the current needs of farmers, residents, and the environment. The region's burgeoning population also puts strains on the local environment, but there is a strong push to protect wetlands from encroaching development.

While all five of the hikes in this section are worthy of exploration in their own right, three of them—the Blue Heron Trails in Stone Lakes National Wildlife Refuge and the River Walk Trail and Wetlands Walk and Boardwalk Trails in Cosumnes River Preserve— are very near I-5 and make excellent stops when you're traveling to points south. Whether you're an avid or casual bird-watcher, you'll definitely want to check out the River Walk Trail, where tens of thousands of migratory waterfowl in fall and winter and many species of songbirds in spring and summer feed and find shelter.

22 **Blue Heron Trails**

DISTANCE:	0.7 mile of trails
ELEVATION GAIN:	Negligible
HIGH POINT:	13 feet
DIFFICULTY:	Easy
FITNESS:	Walkers
FAMILY-FRIENDLY:	Yes, with several educational kiosks and a play area
DOG-FRIENDLY:	No
BIKE-FRIENDLY:	No
AMENITIES:	Restroom by parking area
CONTACT/MAP:	Stone Lakes National Wildlife Refuge; map on sign near trailhead
GPS:	N 38°22.195', W 121°29.730'
MORE KEY INFO:	Open just after sunrise to just before sunset; wheelchair accessible; bird numbers highest Oct.–May; protect wildlife by staying on trails

GETTING THERE

Driving: On I-5 about 15 miles south of downtown Sacramento, take exit 504 and turn right on Hood-Franklin Road. (If you're coming from the south, turn left.) Go west 0.9 mile on Hood-Franklin Road and then turn left at the sign for Stone Lakes National Wildlife Refuge. Follow parking signs to the spacious paved lot.

Although adults certainly appreciate the Blue Heron Trails at Stone Lakes National Wildlife Refuge, the compact trail system and its information kiosks are specifically tailored to the younger crowd. Regardless of your age, you can't beat an opportunity for walking in nature that is a two-minute drive from I-5. Whether or not you bring kiddos, you'll enjoy the plant life and wildlife viewing opportunities.

GET MOVING

Find the concrete trail just beyond the restrooms. Immediately encounter a kiosk with a detailed map of the trail system you'll be exploring as well as important information about local wildlife. The main loop trail begins here. It's almost impossible to get lost in such a compact area, so although this hike description gives specific directions, you can also wander where you will along the trail. But if you want to make sure you don't miss anything, read on.

Turn right and start the loop counterclockwise. Planted in recent years, the vegetation here will take time to mature and provide significant shade. Prominent tree species include

Stone Lakes is one of many national wildlife refuges in the United States.

valley oak, box elder, and blue elderberry, with willows and cottonwoods in the wetter areas.

The immature plant life makes it easy to see distant mountains and hills. You'll appreciate the unobstructed eastward view of the Sierra Nevada, with the upper portion blanketed in snow for most of the year. You'll also have an open westward vista of the Coast Range, with Mount Diablo prominent on the southwest horizon.

Pass thickets of California wild rose and some native grasses to reach the first information kiosk. As with the other three kiosks you'll encounter, this one has two panels specifically designed to engage kids from kindergarten age through sixth grade in learning about the natural world.

The Little Green Heron Playscape is on the right just beyond the first kiosk. It is a fenced-in area where children can run along the paths, jump on rocks, and explore.

Hop back on the main trail and as you pass Discovery Wetland, on the left, listen for the deep croak of bullfrogs and the high trill of red-winged blackbirds. A path soon branches off on the left. Take this to the first of two wooden bridges, an excellent place to pause and take in the lush vegetation of tules and cattails in Discovery Wetland and to look for frogs, turtles, and river otters. (Both the Discovery Wetland and the nearby Dragonfly Wetland have water year-round.)

The second information kiosk sits just beyond the first bridge on a small island. From the island take another bridge to the amphitheater in the center of the Blue Heron trail system. When you're ready, head back the way you came to the main loop trail.

Just as you resume the counterclockwise loop, another trail branches off to the right: the Lost Coyote Loop. Go right to follow the Lost Coyote Loop as it travels northeast through open grasslands that give the best mountain views so far. It passes by coyote bush, young valley oaks, and an assortment of wildflowers in spring. The Blue Heron Wetland lies to

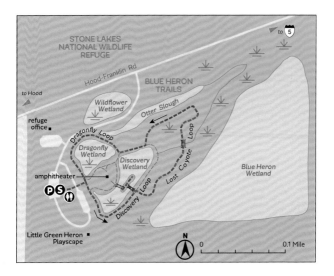

the right; it's an excellent spot to see migrating waterfowl and sandhill cranes from late fall to early spring.

Pass under powerlines and cross a small stream on a wooden bridge before reaching the third information kiosk. Look for the compass impressed into the cement; stand in the middle and verify that you have a good sense of direction. The Lost Coyote Loop then curves west with a full view of the Coast Range beyond the Delta and Sacramento Valley. As you parallel Otter Slough you'll pass a few bird boxes and then rejoin the main loop trail beside a California sycamore.

Turn right to arrive at the fourth information kiosk, this one located between Discovery Wetland and Dragonfly Wetland. A trail leads to the amphitheater; follow it if you want a direct route back to the parking lot. Otherwise take the main route to the right. It passes Otter Slough before curving beside the entrance road and the refuge office to close the loop at the first trail junction of the walk. Turn right for the short return to the parking area.

23   **River Walk Trail**

DISTANCE:	3.8 miles roundtrip
ELEVATION GAIN:	Negligible
HIGH POINT:	15 feet
DIFFICULTY:	Easy
FITNESS:	Walkers
FAMILY-FRIENDLY:	Yes
DOG-FRIENDLY:	No
BIKE-FRIENDLY:	No
AMENITIES:	Bathrooms in lower parking lot and at visitor center; nonmotorized boating on Cosumnes River
CONTACT/MAP:	Cosumnes River Preserve; download map and nature trail guide from website
GPS:	N 38°15.953', W 121°26.389'
MORE KEY INFO:	Trails open sunrise to sunset; can be flooded in winter; visitor center usually open on weekends; migratory birds Oct.–May; trailside poison oak

GETTING THERE

Driving: On I-5 about 21 miles south of downtown Sacramento, take exit 498 and turn left on Twin Cities Road. (Turn right if coming from the south.) Drive east 0.8 mile and then turn right on Franklin Boulevard, just before the railroad tracks. Head south 1.8 miles and then turn left into the Cosumnes River Preserve. Park in the lot farthest east and closest to the visitor center.

A partnership of seven public and private agencies, the Cosumnes River Preserve extends over 50,000 acres in the San Joaquin Valley. The area featured here is easily accessed from I-5 and offers a wide variety of plant habitats, including along the Cosumnes River, where you'll see many different bird species, especially during the winter migration season.

Note that the trails fork a lot. This hike follows the numbering of the first twenty-three posts of the nature trail. Download the trail guide ahead of time to help with navigation, or grab one at the visitor center if it's open. You can also keep your bearings by noting the location of the railroad tracks and the Cosumnes River.

GET MOVING

First head over to the visitor center. Make sure to spend at least a few minutes exploring its fascinating exhibits about local natural and human history.

Willow Slough supports lush vegetation.

To find the trail, look for the prominent sign for the Wetlands Walk and River Walk Trails on the left as you face the visitor center with the parking lot at your back. The two trails share a boardwalk and bridge as they go east for the first 0.1 mile, passing posts 1 through 3. You'll definitely want to stop

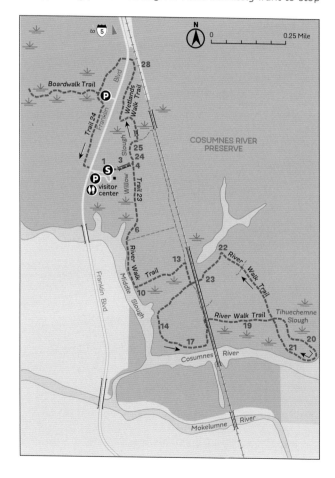

on the bridge over Willow Slough to absorb the lush green-ery of willows and cottonwoods, and to look for great egrets, great blue herons, pond turtles, and a variety of other birds and wildlife.

Reach a trail fork near post 4 just beyond the trees on the far side of Willow Slough. Trail 24 (Wetlands Walk and Boardwalk Trails) goes left, but you go right on the River Walk Trail. The way now heads south on a dirt path. Lush greenery borders Willow Slough on the right; to the left lie managed wetlands that are flooded in winter to provide habitat for migrating waterfowl but are dry from spring through late fall.

A path forks left at 0.4 mile between posts 6 and 7; stay straight on the main route. The easterly vista includes cotton-woods, willows, valley oaks, and railroad tracks. Soon reach a viewpoint of Middle Slough, much larger than Willow Slough and another good place to pause and watch the wildlife. Continuing, note a freshwater seasonal marsh on the left, and then reach a fork at 0.6 mile, where you stick to the River Walk Trail.

As you walk along a seasonal marsh bordered by cattails, look for migrating ducks and geese in winter, and great blue herons, great white herons, and red-winged blackbirds the rest of the year.

Arrive at another junction at 0.8 mile, near the railroad tracks and post 13. Turn right and go south 0.1 mile to another junction, where you again go right. Walk west by southwest and then due south to a valley oak grove and post 14 at 1.2 miles.

Curve southeast to reach post 17 at 1.4 miles. Leave the main path and take the short path to the right that takes you to the banks of the Cosumnes River, a beautiful spot to stand or sit in the shade and watch the water flow. The Cosumnes River begins in the High Sierra south of Lake Tahoe in El Dorado County and flows about 53 miles through the Sierra foothills and the San Joaquin Valley to end at the Mokelumne

River just a half mile downstream; it's one of the few Sierra Nevada rivers with no significant dams.

Return to the main path and go right (east) for 0.1 mile, and then curve north and walk near the railroad tracks for another 0.1 mile to a trail fork at 1.6 miles. Go right (east) to pass under the railroad tracks. Continue east through extensive oak savanna and past post 19 to yet another junction at 1.9 miles.

Head straight across and continue briefly east and then southeast to post 20 at 2.1 miles, where Tihuechemne Slough meets the Cosumnes River, a favorite spot for great white egrets and great blue herons. Go westerly near the banks of the Cosumnes River to post 21 and a rare (for here) live oak tree before walking north to close the loop at 2.4 miles at the most recently encountered trail junction.

At this trail junction go straight (northerly) across the open savanna to meet another broad path at 2.6 miles. Continue straight, walking northwest to post 22 at 2.7 miles, where you'll see magnificent valley oaks and a tule marsh frequented by red-winged blackbirds.

From here, the route goes southwest 0.2 mile to post 23 and the railroad tracks, which you walk under. You are now back on previously walked trail. Go north 0.1 mile to the junction near post 13, turn left and walk west to post 10, near Middle Slough, and then turn right to walk north back to post 4. Turn left to cross the bridge over Willow Slough and return to the trailhead.

GO FARTHER

The obvious choice is the Wetlands Walk and Boardwalk Trails (Trail 24). Join it at post 4 of the nature trail beside the bridge across Willow Slough, walking north from the bridge. Since you're already on the far side of the bridge, this option adds 1.5 miles if you do all of Trail 24, or 1.0 mile if you skip the half-mile roundtrip jaunt on the Boardwalk Trail.

24 Wetlands Walk and Boardwalk Trails

DISTANCE:	1.6 miles roundtrip
ELEVATION GAIN:	Negligible
HIGH POINT:	15 feet
DIFFICULTY:	Easy
FITNESS:	Walkers
FAMILY-FRIENDLY:	Yes
DOG-FRIENDLY:	No
BIKE-FRIENDLY:	No
AMENITIES:	Bathrooms in lower parking lot and at visitor center; nonmotorized boating on Cosumnes River
CONTACT/MAP:	Cosumnes River Preserve; download map and nature trail guide from website
GPS:	N 38°15.953', W 121°26.389'
MORE KEY INFO:	Trails open sunrise to sunset; Boardwalk Trail open 10 AM to 4 PM; visitor center usually open on weekends; wheelchair accessible

GETTING THERE

Driving: On I-5 about 21 miles south of downtown Sacramento, take exit 498 and turn left on Twin Cities Road. (Turn right if you're coming from the south.) Drive east 0.8 mile and then turn right on Franklin Boulevard, just before the railroad tracks. Head south 1.8 miles and then turn left into the Cosumnes River Preserve. Park in the lot farthest east and closest to the visitor center.

This **ADA-compliant loop trail** makes it easy for just about everyone to enjoy the beauty of Cosumnes River Preserve. It takes you along willow-lined sloughs and past seasonal wetlands, the latter covered with thousands of migratory birds in late fall and winter. In addition, you'll win vistas of the Sierra Nevada and the Coast Range, including Mount Diablo.

Great egrets are spectacular birds found at Cosumnes River Preserve.

GET MOVING

Start near the visitor center, which has displays that show common birds in the San Joaquin and Sacramento Valleys. The trail begins to the left of the visitor center as you face it with the parking lot to your back; you'll see the sign for the Wetlands Walk Trail and the River Walk Trail (Trail 23). The wooden boardwalk runs east to a bridge spanning Willow Slough. Pause here and observe the still waters and winged wildlife of the willow-bordered slough. Signs explain that the slough's water level rises and falls in tandem with the ocean tides—the elevation here is only five feet.

When you're ready, continue east to a trail junction at 0.1 mile. The River Walk Trail goes to the right, but you turn left and wander north. On the left are valley oaks that border the banks of Willow Slough. On the right a seasonal marsh stretches east to the railroad tracks; you'll spot distant willows and cottonwoods growing in places with summer moisture, and you'll also spy the occasional valley oak.

On the left at post 24 is a pole with a nesting box for tree swallows; as you continue, if you look closely in the trees, you'll also see nesting boxes for wood ducks. Just beyond post 24 a picnic table rests underneath oak shade.

At post 25 at 0.2 mile a small side trail on the left runs 100 feet into a grove of valley oaks. The main trail swings briefly right (east) and then curves left to resume its northerly course. Reach and then cross a bridge across Willow Slough, noting the many tules that grow in and near the willow-lined slough.

Once past Willow Slough the route runs west and then north through oak savanna. The valley oaks here, planted by volunteers in 1988, are still quite small; as a result, from here until the end of the hike there is almost no shade. Travel beside a smaller slough lined with lush vegetation and past a trailside bench to another bench beside a year-round pond and post 28 at 0.5 mile. The pond is an excellent spot to watch wildlife; look for turtles, river otters, great blue herons, and more.

The path is now sandwiched between the railroad tracks on the right and Franklin Boulevard on the left, but it soon heads left (west) to cross Franklin Boulevard. (Watch children closely since traffic does not stop for pedestrians.)

Now on the west side of Franklin Boulevard, the trail begins a long southerly run past more benches, offering opportunities to enjoy a clear view to the west of the hills and mountains of the Coast Range, anchored by Mount Diablo to the southwest. Franklin Boulevard runs close by on the left (east), with a seasonal pond on the right. Flooded in fall and winter, the pond provides prime habitat for majestic sandhill cranes. These graceful birds with a wingspan of up to seven feet are making a strong comeback in the Central Valley.

Arrive at the parking lot for the Boardwalk Trail at 0.7 mile. Take the boardwalk west, passing seasonal wetlands filled with tules and willows and, in spring and early summer, wild-flowers. The Boardwalk Trail ends at a viewing platform. When you turn around for the return to the main trail, you'll see the distant Sierra Nevada to the east, crested by snow from late fall well into summer.

Return to the Boardwalk Trail parking lot at 1.2 miles. Turn right to resume hiking on the Wetlands Walk Trail. As you continue south, you'll see a small slough on the left and a seasonal wetland on the right until the path swings east at 1.5 miles to cross Franklin Boulevard and return you to the parking lot and your vehicle.

GO FARTHER

If you want to move more after completing the loop, stroll again along the boardwalk to the bridge across Willow Slough, continue beyond to the trail fork, and then go right for the River Walk Trail (Trail 23).

25 Lodi Lake Nature Trail

DISTANCE:	1.3-mile loop
ELEVATION GAIN:	Negligible
HIGH POINT:	50 feet
DIFFICULTY:	Easy
FITNESS:	Walkers, runners
FAMILY-FRIENDLY:	Yes
DOG-FRIENDLY:	No
BIKE-FRIENDLY:	Yes, on paved path and wide dirt path by levee
AMENITIES:	Bathrooms, picnic tables, and water at trailhead and other parts of Lodi Lake Park
CONTACT/MAP:	Lodi Parks and Recreation; map on sign at trailhead
GPS:	N 38˚8.906', W 121˚17.524'
MORE KEY INFO:	Open sunrise to sunset daily; fee; wheelchair accessible; swimming in lake in summer

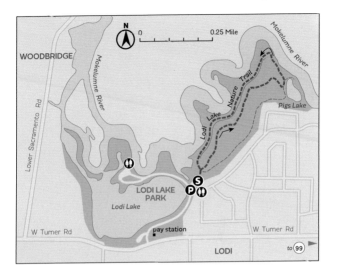

GETTING THERE

Driving: Drive Highway 99 south about 35 miles from downtown Sacramento and take exit 267A, signed for Turner Road. Go left at the stop sign onto East Turner Road. Follow East Turner Road, which becomes West Turner Road at North Sacramento Street, 1.7 miles and then turn right into Lodi Lake Park. The pay station for the entrance fee is immediately to your right. Follow the main road to the right beside Lodi Lake for 0.2 mile and then turn right into the trailhead parking lot. If the parking lot is full, return to the main park road and continue another 100 yards around the lake to the parking lot just past the park entrance.

    Transit: Bus 1 on weekdays and Buses 1 and 30 on weekends stop at Lodi Lake Park.

This beautiful nature loop trail provides welcome wilderness for Lodi residents and visitors. Its many trees shield most traffic and town noise, allowing hikers, runners, and bikers to hear

Refreshing shade along the flat, paved Lodi Lake Nature Trail

birdsong. This is also a great place to spot deer or a fox and to sit beside a meander of the Mokelumne River and watch the water slowly flow by.

GET MOVING

First read the murals that explain the natural and human history of the Mokelumne River. Note the wide dirt path to the right (see Go Farther) and then go straight on the paved path. Just 50 feet beyond the murals the trail forks beside a sign that shows the locations of the numbered interpretive signs.

You'll return via the left-hand dirt path, but for now go straight on the paved path.

The small interpretive signs provide excellent details of the many facets of natural history you encounter on the hike, including the small grove of peaceful redwoods just beyond the fork. Walk under the shade of live oaks and past non-native black locust trees, with large quantities of nonnative Himalaya blackberry in the understory.

At 0.2 mile encounter the first of several trailside benches, this one near a willow tree, an indication of the high water table here near the Mokelumne River. Just beyond the bench a short path goes left to connect to the other part of the loop trail. Continue straight along the flat and shaded path to the end of the pavement at 0.5 mile.

Walk the now-dirt path to four yellow posts, with Pigs Lake just beyond. The main route of the hike curves left. You'll also see a dirt path coming in on the right, which is described in Go Farther. Go straight on the short side path to Pigs Lake to watch birds flying across the water and flitting in the bordering trees and shrubs.

When you're ready, continue along the side path on the left (west) side of Pigs Lake to the bench bordering the Mokelumne River. This is the perfect place to take a short rest and observe the broad stream, which begins as snowmelt on High Sierra peaks, then rushes down steep canyons in the Sierra Nevada. After it enters the Central Valley, it winds slowly through gentle meanders to empty into the San Joaquin River, providing irrigation and drinking water along the way. Look east beyond the river and agricultural lands to see the mighty Sierra far in the distance.

Back on the main trail, walk near the Mokelumne River, with several side trails leading down to the banks. Pass an area filled with water-loving sedges at 0.8 mile and then look across the river to a vineyard. Move away from the river to wander under valley oaks and cottonwoods and past willows;

you'll also see California wild grape growing along the ground and high up tree trunks.

At 0.9 mile, you'll spy a small slough filled with cattails on the left, and then the trail again reaches the banks of the Mokelumne River, allowing good views of cottonwoods and valley oaks on the far side. At 1.1 miles again approach the river for a good view of the water with cottonwood trees beyond on the far bank, followed soon by the short connector trail on the left that you encountered at 0.2 mile near the first bench. Continue on the main path to close the loop at 1.3 miles near the murals and trailhead.

GO FARTHER

From the murals near the trailhead, take the wide dirt path on the right. It runs a half mile below a levee and near houses to meet the main hiking loop at the four yellow posts near Pigs Lake. You can also walk around much of Lodi Lake, including along the beach.

26 | Howard Ranch Trail

DISTANCE:	7.1 miles roundtrip
ELEVATION GAIN:	100 feet
HIGH POINT:	300 feet
DIFFICULTY:	Easy to moderate
FITNESS:	Walkers, runners
FAMILY-FRIENDLY:	Yes
DOG-FRIENDLY:	No
BIKE-FRIENDLY:	No
AMENITIES:	Restroom at trailhead
CONTACT/MAP:	Sacramento Municipal Utilities District; download map from website
GPS:	N 38°20.418', W 121°5.801'
MORE KEY INFO:	Open 7 AM to 3:30 PM Nov.–Mar., 7 AM to 6 PM Apr.–Oct.; fee

GETTING THERE

Driving: Drive Highway 99 south from Sacramento about 21 miles and then take the Highway 104 and Twin Cities Road exit (exit 277). Head east on Highway 104 (Twin Cities Road) and at 12.4 miles turn right at the sign for Rancho Seco Park. Go 0.3 mile on the main road and then turn left at the Rancho Seco Recreational Area sign. Pass the entrance station, go another 0.5 mile, and then near Rancho Seco Lake, turn left onto a gravel road signed for the Howard Ranch Trail. Continue another 0.3 mile to the trailhead.

The Howard Ranch Trail is most attractive on a clear spring day when wildflowers are in full bloom, the snowcapped Sierra commands the eastern view, and ephemeral vernal pools dot the landscape. Fall and winter along Rancho Seco Lake offer their own beauty, but summers here are hot and dry, and most of the trail is fully exposed to the sun.

GET MOVING

The Howard Ranch Trail begins by the large signboard at the northeast edge of the parking lot. The path initially runs near the north shore of Rancho Seco Lake, at times on boardwalk to help protect sensitive plants. Cottonwoods and willows line the shore, providing greenery in spring and summer and beautiful yellows in autumn. Several small paths lead down to the water, where anglers frequently try their luck.

Spot red-winged blackbirds plus ducks, geese, and other water-loving birds as you continue. You'll also see the campgrounds, picnic areas, and other recreation facilities on the built-up portion of Rancho Seco Recreational Area on the lake's southwest shore. If you glance west, you'll spy the cooling towers of the decommissioned Rancho Seco nuclear power plant; first brought online in 1975, it was shut down permanently by a 1989 referendum after a series of safety incidents, shutdowns, and cost overruns.

Cross two small bridges across two small seasonal streams at 1.1 miles, and at the northeast tip of the lake, then reach a gate beside a ranch road at 1.2 miles. Go through the gate (make sure to close it behind you) and cross the road to continue on the hiking trail. You're now on open, gentle slopes of privately owned Howard Ranch, which was purchased in the 1930s by Charles Howard, the owner of the famous race-horse Seabiscuit. The Nature Conservancy bought the ranch in 1999, placed covenants on its use to protect the local environment, and then resold the land to a cattle rancher.

You'll see cattle for much of the remainder of the hike. Walk northeast and enjoy a view of the distant Sierra Nevada, snowcapped throughout most of the year. The way passes numerous vernal pools. These small, shallow depressions fill with winter rainwater, when they harbor endangered species like fairy shrimp. After the pools dry out later in spring, your eye will be treated to small wildflower blooms, including yellow carpet, meadowfoam, and sky blues; this is prime territory for a variety of spring wildflowers. You'll also likely see

California poppies brighten the Howard Ranch Trail.

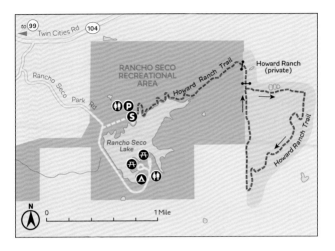

the yellow flash of flying meadowlarks and hear their distinctive multitone song.

The route curves right to head south. It passes through another gate at 1.9 miles (close it behind you), and then reaches a trail fork at 2.1 miles, the beginning of the loop portion of the hike. Go left and head east toward the distant Sierra Nevada, passing just south of three small ponds and many mounds of dredge tailings plus a few cottonwood trees.

The trail turns south beside a fence at 2.6 miles. After a brief jog west, it runs southwesterly and then south along the top of a rim, with vistas of oak-dotted Sierra Nevada foothills. It meets a ranch road beside a fence at 4.0 miles. Turn right (north) on the ranch road and start a long, straight stretch beside the fence, only curving slightly away between 4.4 and 4.6 miles.

Close the loop at 5.0 miles. From here, go 2.1 miles back the way you came, north and then west to return to the trailhead.

Next page: *Valley oaks thrive in the rich soils near Putah Creek.*

WEST OF SACRAMENTO

Agricultural land dominates the Sacramento Valley to the west of Sacramento, and Davis is the main town in the region. Still a moderately sized city, Davis is best known for its University of California campus, which started as an agricultural college in 1908 and has since grown into one of the highest-ranked academic institutions in the United States.

Residents and visitors to Davis have many hiking opportunities. Just east of town and south of I-80 stretches the Yolo Bypass Wildlife Area, which serves both as a repository for winter and spring stormwaters and as an important refuge for birds and animals; two hikes explore this area.

You'll also find two walks in Davis itself: the Covell Greenbelt, a favorite with locals, plus the well-known UC Davis Arboretum, on the southern part of the campus along the former channel of Putah Creek. The nearby Putah Creek Riparian Reserve lies just outside the town boundaries. Ranging farther west, the bucolic town of Winters features trails on and near levees bordering Putah Creek. And the westernmost hikes in the book run in and near the UC Davis Stebbins Cold Canyon Reserve near Putah Creek and Lake Berryessa in the foothills of the Coast Range.

27 Cache Creek Nature Preserve

DISTANCE:	2.0 miles of trails
ELEVATION GAIN:	Up to 100 feet
HIGH POINT:	110 feet
DIFFICULTY:	Easy
FITNESS:	Walkers, runners
FAMILY-FRIENDLY:	Yes
DOG-FRIENDLY:	On-leash
BIKE-FRIENDLY:	No
AMENITIES:	Restrooms, picnic tables, visitor center
CONTACT/MAP:	Cache Creek Nature Preserve; download map from website or obtain at visitor center
GPS:	N 38˚41.355', W 121˚52.386'
MORE KEY INFO:	Open Mon.–Fri., 8 AM to 4 PM, plus some weekends (call ahead)

GETTING THERE

Driving: From Sacramento, take I-5 north to Woodland, taking exit 541, signed for Highway 16 and Esparto. Turn left onto Highway 16 West (also Pedrick Road, or County Road 98). Go south 2.7 miles to a stoplight, and go right to continue on Highway 16. Drive west on Highway 16 for 2.7 miles, and then bear right onto CR 22. After another 0.9 mile, go right on CR 94B. Drive 1.0 mile and turn left on CR 20. Continue another 0.4 mile to find the Cache Creek Nature Preserve on the left. Follow the main entrance road 0.2 mile and then park on the left.

The Jan T. Lowrey Cache Creek Nature Preserve packs a plethora of natural beauty into its 130 acres. The preserve includes extensive wetlands, lowlands near Cache Creek that flood frequently in winter, and uplands dotted with valley oaks that burst with wildflowers in spring. This preserve is a great

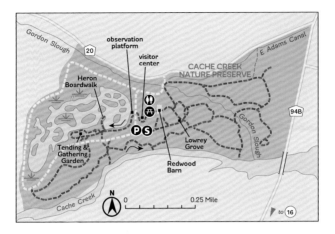

place to explore with kids; numerous informational signs describe human and natural history, and there's plenty for kids to see and do.

GET MOVING

First spend a bit of time at the visitor center, where you'll learn a lot about the preserve and can also grab the trail map. The preserve owes much to its namesake, Jan T. Lowrey, who passed away in 2006. One of the founding board members of the Cache Creek Conservancy, Lowrey served as its first executive director and was instrumental in all facets of its design and development.

An extensive network of trails interlaces the preserve. You can follow them where you'd like since it's almost impossible to get lost. Rather than lead you along a specific itinerary of paths, this description will highlight the main features and provide a suggested sequence for your explorations.

The wetlands immediately west of the parking lot and visitor center will almost certainly catch your eye first. A viewpoint just north of the parking lot and beside the entrance

Redbud and wetlands in Cache Creek Nature Preserve

road is a great place to start; here redbuds frame a vista of the wetlands and the foothills of the Coast Range on the west side of the Sacramento Valley.

You'll spy an observation deck below in the wetlands; either take the trail directly to it or arc around on the road on the main levee. The Heron Boardwalk, which features plaques with resident bird names and pictures, leads to the observation platform. Here you can watch Canada geese, coots, a variety of ducks, great blue herons, and an assortment of other waterbirds going about their daily business.

Take the path farther west along the wetlands to the Tending and Gathering Garden. Here you can sit in the shade of the ramada and read how the Wintun tribe made use of various plants and managed natural habitats.

Climb up to the levee and continue west by southwest to approach the boundary of the preserve. Then drop south to the dirt path that runs easterly near the banks of willow- and cottonwood-lined Cache Creek; this major stream runs from Clear Lake to the Sacramento River, providing irrigation water and recreational opportunities along the way. This path can flood during and after winter and spring storms; as a result, it can be quite muddy during those seasons.

The path near Cache Creek eventually brings you to Lowrey Grove, which features an amphitheater and a variety of natural plant species. Trails continue easterly amid valley oaks. If Gordon Slough is dry, you can cross to the northeast section of the preserve to explore more oak woodland habitat.

Also visit the Redwood Barn, located between the visitor center and Lowrey Grove. It houses an antique combine harvester and a variety of other old farm equipment. Grab your lunch or a snack and settle in at one of the picnic tables here for a peaceful respite.

28 Yolo Bypass Wildlife Area: Pond Walk

DISTANCE:	1.8 miles roundtrip
ELEVATION GAIN:	Negligible
HIGH POINT:	10 feet
DIFFICULTY:	Easy
FITNESS:	Walkers
FAMILY-FRIENDLY:	Yes
DOG-FRIENDLY:	No
BIKE-FRIENDLY:	No
AMENITIES:	Restrooms at trailhead and at Parking Lot B
CONTACT/MAP:	Yolo Bypass Wildlife Area; download map from website
GPS:	N 38˚33.035', W 121˚37.574'
MORE KEY INFO:	Open sunrise to sunset daily, except Christmas and when flooded after heavy rain; gate locked daily at sunset; most birds Dec.–Mar.

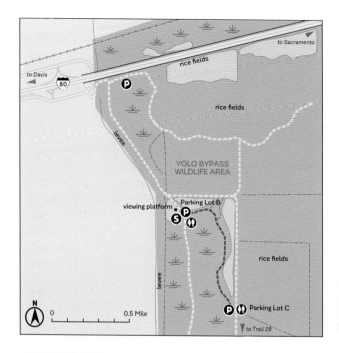

GETTING THERE

Driving: Take I-80 about 8 miles west of downtown Sacramento (or 3 miles east of Davis) and take the East Chiles Road exit (exit 78). Once you're on the south side of the freeway, reset your trip odometer to zero, and take the first gravel road on the left, signed for Yolo Bypass Wildlife Area. Drive up and over the levee and turn right on the first gravel road at 0.2 mile. Go right at 1.0 mile and continue another 0.2 mile to the trailhead at Parking Lot B.

Many people frequently drive I-80 between Davis and Sacramento and notice that vast expanse of land south of the freeway—a mix of dry uplands, seasonal marshes, and permanent wetlands, with vast flocks of geese in the winter. Just a couple of minutes off the freeway, this easy trail in the Yolo Bypass Wildlife Area between Parking Lot B and Parking Lot C lets you explore the biological diversity of this special place.

GET MOVING

Start your explorations by first going back 200 feet on the road to the wheelchair-accessible viewing platform on the left. Stroll 100 feet out to the end, which borders the edge of a permanent wetland. This is an ideal spot for observing a wide variety of birds, with by far the most impressive display from December through March, when thousands upon thousands of migrating geese and ducks take advantage of this prime habitat. If you're lucky, you'll see a huge flock of snow geese rise from the water to whirl above you in the sky.

American coots are common in Yolo Bypass Wildlife Area.

Return to Parking Lot B and find the beginning of the trail on the east side. Start walking east on the broad levee, which is mowed in the warmer seasons. Pass a seasonal pond on the left; it's filled with water during the rainy season, but the wildlife area managers let it dry out in summer. Its mud-flats are a favorite haunt of American avocets, who poke their long beaks into the mud to snack on insects. Stay to the right at 0.1 mile at a meeting with another levee road. There's some traffic noise from nearby I-80, but the wind and birdsong drown most of it out, and it fades during the course of the walk as you venture farther south and away from the freeway.

The trail begins arcing to the right and soon the route runs south, the direction it maintains for the rest of the hike. Pause here to take in the vistas that stretch in all directions beyond the flatness of the Sacramento Valley. On especially clear days your eyes will be drawn east to the Sierra Nevada, snowcapped the entire year, except in late summer and early autumn. Coast Range hills rise above the western edge of the valley, running from the distant north down to prominent Mount Diablo in the south.

A range of plants border the trail as you continue, including numerous wildflowers in spring. In summer look for the purple flowers of field mint. Reach down and lightly brush it with your hand and then enjoy the sharp and invigorating scent. You'll soon see a year-round pond on the left, which hosts thickets of reeds as well as numerous cattails. This is the perfect habitat for red-winged blackbirds; you'll see them flitting from stalk to stalk, and you'll definitely hear their melodic trill.

Reach Parking Lot C at 0.9 mile, the turnaround point of the hike. From here, retrace your steps back to the trailhead at Parking Lot B.

29 Yolo Bypass Wildlife Area Loop

DISTANCE:	2.3-mile loop
ELEVATION GAIN:	Negligible
HIGH POINT:	10 feet
DIFFICULTY:	Easy
FITNESS:	Walkers
FAMILY-FRIENDLY:	Yes
DOG-FRIENDLY:	No
BIKE-FRIENDLY:	No
AMENITIES:	Restroom at trailhead
CONTACT/MAP:	Yolo Bypass Wildlife Area; download map from website
GPS:	N 38˚31.784', W 121˚35.400'
MORE KEY INFO:	Open sunrise to sunset, early Feb. to mid-Oct., except when flooded after heavy rain; gate locked at sunset; closed rest of year

GETTING THERE

Driving: Take I-80 about 8 miles west of downtown Sacramento (or 3 miles east of Davis) and take the East Chiles Road exit (exit 78). Once on the south side of the freeway, reset your trip odometer to zero, and take the first gravel road on the left, signed for Yolo Bypass Wildlife Area. Drive up and over the levee and turn right on the first gravel road at 0.2 mile. At 1.0 mile at a road junction, follow the main road to the left (going right leads 0.2 mile to the Trail 28 trailhead). The road heads east, then curves south at 1.4 miles, then passes Parking Lot C at 2.2 miles, the far point of Trail 28. At 2.9 miles go left, following signs for Parking Lot F. The road jogs south at 3.3 miles then immediately heads east again; you'll reach the trailhead at Parking Lot F at 4.6 miles.

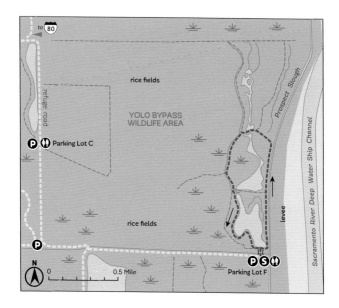

Wander along willow-lined ponds, saunter beside tranquil sloughs, and enjoy abundant avian wildlife on this easy hike in the Yolo Bypass Wildlife Area, located between Davis and West Sacramento. Bonus: The drive to the trailhead takes you through many beautiful parts of the wildlife area.

GET MOVING
Head to the northwest corner of the parking lot and begin the hike by crossing a concrete walkway that spans one of the many sloughs that crisscross the Yolo Bypass Wildlife Area. First opened to the public in 1997, the Yolo Bypass Wildlife Area encompasses over 16,000 acres of permanent ponds, seasonal wetlands, and upland areas. It's a haven for wildlife and also serves a flood-control function during heavy precipitation years, when the land here is flooded and access is prohibited.

While on the bridge over the slough, stop to observe the water and take advantage of the open vistas: Mount Diablo anchors the southernmost view, with lesser Coast Range ridges and peaks extending along the west side of the Sacramento Valley to fade out of sight far to the north.

Once on the far side of the concrete walkway, go right on the levee road, noting that you'll be returning from the left at the end of the hike. Continue east with a permanent pond on your left that's ringed by cattails, reeds, and willows. Stop here for a few minutes and quietly observe the bird life. If it's winter, you'll see vast numbers of snow geese and other migrating birds taking advantage of the warmer temperatures and abundant food before winging north in spring to raise young in the higher latitudes of Canada and Alaska. There are dozens of year-round residents (search for bird lists online), and you'll always see red-winged blackbirds and yellow-billed magpies, along with Canada geese, mallard ducks, double-breasted cormorants, and great blue herons.

When you're ready, continue east another 100 yards and then curve north at 0.1 mile. A larger slough is now on your right, with a levee on the far side that blocks eastward views. The Sacramento River Deep Water Ship Channel is just out of sight on the other side of the levee; it begins at the Port of Sacramento in West Sacramento and runs south 43 miles to connect to the Sacramento River, allowing large ships to travel to and from San Francisco Bay. You may pass a few people fishing here, but you soon have a lot of privacy while hawks and vultures circle above. Invasive field bindweed grows low to the ground with its whitish flowers, and in summer you'll see numerous yellow sunflowers. You may hear the low hum of distant traffic on I-80, but birdsong will likely drown it out.

At 0.5 mile a fainter levee road heads left and due west; continue straight and north, paralleling Prospect Slough. The vegetation on the west side soon opens up to reveal willow-framed views of a large pond; this is a good spot to observe great white egrets.

Be watching for a large ditch on the left at 0.9 mile that may have water or may be dry, depending on the lateness of the season. Dirt roads run westerly on both sides of this ditch; turn left on whichever one suits your fancy. Walk past cottonwoods and then between two permanent ponds, another good place for bird-watching.

Whichever road you chose, they both dead-end at 1.1 miles at another road. Turn left and walk southwest toward distant Mount Diablo. The bordering fields can be flooded in winter, damp in spring, and dry brown in summer, and the open country allows full westerly views of the Coast Range west of nearby Davis.

Reach a road junction at 1.5 miles and go left. Reach another junction at 1.7 miles and again go left, almost immediately reaching the edge of a large pond. Saunter south,

Willows and cottonwoods ring the ponds along the loop trail.

stopping frequently to watch the many birds on and near the pond's surface.

Enjoy the pond and open views for another 0.6 mile as you walk south. The road then curves left and east, and at 2.1 miles, you'll reach the cement walkway that returns you to the trailhead at Parking Lot F.

30 Covell Greenbelt

DISTANCE:	2.4-mile loop
ELEVATION GAIN:	Negligible
HIGH POINT:	50 feet
DIFFICULTY:	Easy
FITNESS:	Walkers, runners
FAMILY-FRIENDLY:	Yes
DOG-FRIENDLY:	On-leash
BIKE-FRIENDLY:	Yes
AMENITIES:	Bathrooms, picnic tables, playgrounds
CONTACT/MAP:	Davis Parks and Community Services; download map from website
GPS:	N 38˚33.634', W 121˚44.832'
MORE KEY INFO:	Always open; wheelchair-accessible path in greenbelt

GETTING THERE

Driving: In Davis, about 14 miles west of downtown Sacramento, take the Richards Boulevard exit off I-80 (exit 72) and go 0.2 mile northwest from the freeway into downtown Davis. Turn right on First Street, go one block, and then turn left on F Street. Follow F Street 1.3 miles to West Covell Boulevard. Turn left, go 0.1 mile and, just before the pedestrian bridge, turn left into the Davis Community Park parking lot.

Transit: Multiple Unitrans bus lines stop close to the trailhead. The F Line stops at Catalina Drive near West Covell Boulevard.

An appealing stretch of the Covell Greenbelt on a sunny afternoon

Davis is justly famous for being bike and pedestrian friendly. This walk along the Covell Greenbelt demonstrates why it deserves this reputation in spades. This wide, level, and paved path is heavily used by bicyclists, runners, and walkers of all types, from couples holding hands to parents pushing baby strollers with toddlers in tow. Many streets feed into the greenbelt, making it easy for residents and visitors alike to walk as much or as little as they want.

GET MOVING

Use the pedestrian bridge to go north and cross over West Covell Boulevard. Immediately enter Covell Park, a five-acre expanse of green with a children's playground. Reach the first fork at 0.2 mile just beyond the playground; left is your return route; go right to start a long counterclockwise loop. You'll notice the Spanish names of the various streets and cul-de-sacs that border the greenbelt and allow access. Some are named for people—Cortez, Balboa, Benicia; some are named for places—Jalisco, Ipanema; and some invoke ideas, objects, and concepts—Diablo (devil), Faro (lighthouse), Estrella (star).

Continue along the east side of Covell Park to tennis courts (with nearby bathrooms) at 0.4 mile. There's another junction here; stay to the right to walk along a narrower corridor amply shaded from spring through autumn, eventually crossing Grande Avenue at 0.6 mile. Feel like sitting and just enjoying the tranquil surroundings? Take advantage of the many benches in this stretch and all along the greenbelt.

You'll hear geese and ducks and then see Julie Partansky Pond on the right at 0.8 mile in Northstar Park. Partansky was a Davis city council member and mayor; the pond is named in her memory. Take the boardwalk 200 feet out to the viewing platform. Here you can sit on benches and watch the many birds living their lives on and near the willow-ringed waters.

The path leaves Julie Partansky Pond to curve west through Northstar Park (look for restrooms just to the north, on the right) and arc around a smaller pond. Listen for the distinctive trill of red-winged blackbirds and look for their red patches as they flit among cattails. Canada geese also frequent this second pond; look for them out on the water and also feeding on the grass near the path.

Head briefly south and look for an informational signboard on the right at 1.1 miles, just before a playground. The signboard announces the Northstar Nature Garden; here you turn right to walk west on the dirt path that passes through multiple arbors as it runs near a soccer field. The dirt path rejoins the nearby paved path at 1.2 miles, which immediately curves south beside another playground.

Cross Catalina Drive at 1.4 miles. As you continue, you'll see three metal statues of dogs at play. The first is

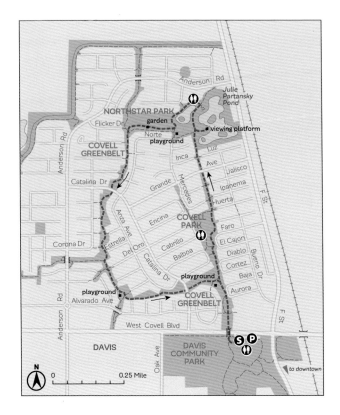

on the right at 1.5 miles: a dog harassing what looks like a goose. You'll see the second shortly thereafter, also on the right; this dog is nosing something on the ground. And the last one on the left is riding a tricycle with his tongue hanging out.

Reach another playground at 1.9 miles, along with a fork. You go left (the right-hand path leads to a tunnel). Cross Catalina Drive at 2.1 miles and reach the close of the loop at 2.2 miles in Covell Park by the playground. Go right for the final 0.2 mile to the pedestrian bridge across West Covell Boulevard and then back to the parking area.

GO FARTHER

Walk more of the greenbelt by taking the section that heads west between Estrella Place and Del Oro Place at 1.7 miles. You can also check out Davis Community Park at the trail-head parking area, or wander the many residential streets surrounding the Covell Greenbelt.

31 UC Davis Arboretum

DISTANCE:	3.5-mile loop, plus 1.0-mile side trail
ELEVATION GAIN:	50 feet
HIGH POINT:	50 feet
DIFFICULTY:	Easy
FITNESS:	Walkers, runners
FAMILY-FRIENDLY:	Yes
DOG-FRIENDLY:	On-leash
BIKE-FRIENDLY:	Yes
AMENITIES:	Restrooms and drinking fountains along route and in university buildings northwest of arboretum
CONTACT/MAP:	UC Davis Arboretum; download map from website
GPS:	N 38˚32.316', W 121˚44.726'
MORE KEY INFO:	Always open; parking fee Mon.–Fri., credit card only, free on weekends; wheelchair accessible

GETTING THERE

Driving: In Davis, about 14 miles west of downtown Sacramento, take the Richards Boulevard exit off I-80 (exit 72). Go 0.2 mile northwest from the freeway into downtown Davis and then curve left onto First Street. Continue 0.2 mile on First Street and then turn left onto Old Davis Road. Pass Parking Lot 10 and go 0.1 mile and then turn left into Parking Lot 5 (visitor parking) just after the Old Davis Road bridge. If driving east on I-80, take the UC Davis Mondavi Center exit (exit 71). Turn left on Old Davis Road, continue 0.9 mile, and then turn right into Parking Lot 5.

Transit: Multiple Unitrans bus lines stop within walking distance of the Arboretum. The A, D, and L lines all stop at Shields Library 100 yards north of the Arboretum's Lake Spafford.

The UC Davis Arboretum hosts numerous collections of plant species from areas of the world that have a climate similar to the Sacramento Valley. Along the 3.5-mile trail encircling the old channel of Putah Creek you'll see hundreds of trees, shrubs, and flowers from Australia, South Africa, and the Mediterranean, as well as many native Californian species.

The Arboretum is popular with students, residents, and visitors, so expect plenty of company. The general route described here begins at Parking Lot 5 along Old Davis Road, but you can access the path from other parking lots and by walking through the UC Davis campus. It's hard to get lost here, and locals are always happy to give you directions, so feel free to pick your own access point and route.

GET MOVING

At 100-plus acres, the UC Davis Arboretum provides a welcome respite for students seeking time away from their studies. It also attracts both locals and visitors who like to wander the mostly shaded paved trail that loops around the old channel of Putah Creek, plus it's the site of research by students and faculty.

Founded in 1936, the Arboretum features more than twenty gardens of plant species from Mediterranean climates around the world, including California, of course, but also Australia, East Asia, Mexico, and the Mediterranean basin itself. The gardens range in scope, from featuring a diversity of plants to, like the Peter J. Shields Oak Grove, focusing on a single species. Some are named for influential figures in the history of the university, such as the aforementioned Shields who was instrumental in the 1906 founding of UC Davis and

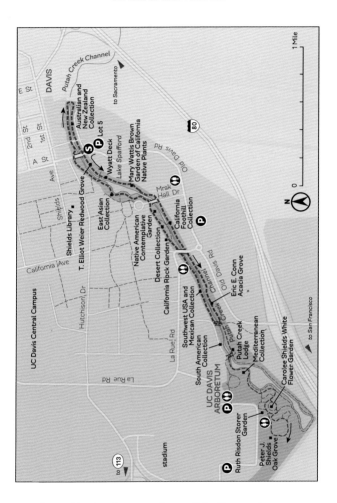

prominent biochemistry professor Eric Conn whose name graces an acacia grove.

Numerous informational signs identify specific plant species and explore different aspects of natural and human history. Of special historical and cultural significance, the Native American Contemplative Garden was dedicated in 2011 as part of the university's efforts to recognize and honor the local Patwin tribe.

Start by heading over to the T. Elliot Weier Redwood Grove, just to the left (west) of the Old Davis Road bridge. Here you'll find the paved path that runs along the southeast side of the Arboretum. Turn left and start a clockwise loop. You're walking beside the old channel of Putah Creek. Davis residents redirected Putah Creek to the south in 1871, and the Army Corps of Engineers built levees in the 1940s to contain it (see Trail 32, Putah Creek Riparian Reserve).

Beyond Wyatt Deck the waterway expands to become Lake Spafford, where you'll see students lounging and studying on the grass on sunny days. Encounter familiar plant

Beauty abounds throughout the UC Davis Arboretum.

species in the Mary Wattis Brown Garden of California Native Plants and farther along the route, at 0.7 mile, at the California Foothill Collection just beyond Mrak Hall Drive.

The path travels beneath the La Rue Road bridge at 1.0 mile. Continue your meandering to the Eric E. Conn Acacia Grove. Shortly beyond, at 1.4 miles, a bridge crosses to the northwest side of the Putah Creek Channel. For the main loop, take this bridge and then turn right on the other side. If you want to add another mile to the 3.5-mile loop, continue along the southeast bank of the channel to Putah Creek Lodge, and then cross the creek and turn left to explore the Carolee Shields White Flower Garden and Gazebo, the Ruth Risdon Storer Garden, and the Peter J. Shields Oak Grove.

Back at the bridge described above at 1.4 miles, continue the main clockwise loop along the northwest bank of the channel. Pass the Southwest USA and Mexican Collection to reach La Rue Road at 1.8 miles; the path again travels under the La Rue Road bridge. Farther along are the California Rock Garden, the Desert Collection, and the Native American Contemplative Garden. Then meet up with Mrak Hall Drive at 2.2 miles.

From Mrak Hall Drive, make your way past the East Asian Collection and the grassy expanse beside Lake Spafford to reach Old Davis Road at 2.9 miles. A right turn here brings you to Parking Lot 5. The loop trail continues on, though, crossing Old Davis Road and then arcing around the far end of the Putah Creek Channel to pass through the Australian and New Zealand Collection before bringing you once again to Old Davis Road at 3.5 miles. Turn left on Old Davis Road to reach Parking Lot 5 and your vehicle.

GO FARTHER

UC Davis is a large and beautiful campus. Wander where you want along the northwest side of the Arboretum.

32

Putah Creek Riparian Reserve

DISTANCE:	2.7 miles of trails
ELEVATION GAIN:	50 feet
HIGH POINT:	70 feet
DIFFICULTY:	Easy
FITNESS:	Walkers, runners
FAMILY-FRIENDLY:	Yes
DOG-FRIENDLY:	On-leash on Levee Road only; not allowed on trail
BIKE-FRIENDLY:	On Levee Road only
AMENITIES:	Restrooms and picnic tables at both trailheads
CONTACT/MAP:	UC Davis Arboretum; download map from website
GPS:	Hopkins Road trailhead: N 38°31.515', W 121°47.399'
	Old Davis Road trailhead: N 38°31.079', W 121°45.387'
MORE KEY INFO:	Open sunrise to sunset; portions of trail submerged during and after major winter storms; Levee Road is always accessible

GETTING THERE

Driving: Take I-80 from downtown Sacramento about 14 miles to its junction with Highway 113 in Davis and go north (exit 70). Immediately take exit 27 for Hutchison Drive. Go left on Hutchison Drive and cross over Highway 113. Negotiate a roundabout and head north to stay on Hutchison Drive, then take another roundabout to continue west. Go 1.0 mile past the second roundabout and then turn left (south) on Hopkins Road. You'll pass various UC Davis facilities and the UC Davis airport; at 0.9 mile the road curves left, where you'll find trailhead parking on the right.

To reach the Old Davis Road trailhead, take the UC Davis Mondavi Center exit off I-80 (exit 71). Turn left (south) on Old Davis Road if coming from Sacramento and right (south) if coming from points west. At about 0.7 mile turn left on gravel Levee Road just before the bridge, and then immediately turn right into the parking lot.

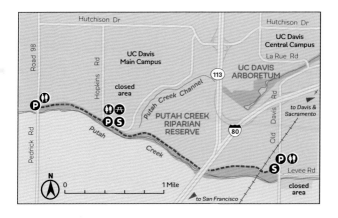

Part of UC Davis and a year-round favorite with Davis residents, this riparian reserve runs along the north side of Putah Creek and includes both a trail near and through riparian areas on the floodplain near the creek (often inaccessible during and after periods of heavy rain) and a levee road with excellent views of Putah Creek and the expanse of Sacramento Valley agricultural land stretching to the bordering hills and mountains. The south side is private property; do not trespass.

GET MOVING

In a region dominated by agriculture, the Putah Creek Riparian Reserve is a haven of native riparian plant life. Near the borders of the creek you'll spy cottonwoods, box elders, and willows, with valley oaks inhabiting the rich soils a bit farther from the creek. Mustard, California poppy, and other wildflowers bloom profusely in spring.

The Putah Creek Riparian Reserve and its associated trail and Levee Road run from Pedrick Road on the west to Old Davis Road on the east. While it's all attractive, the portion that runs near and under I-80 is definitely less so. Walkers and

Valley oaks on the levee beside Putah Creek

runners can use the dirt path or the dirt levee; both paths run near each other most of the way.

If you start at Hopkins Road, you'll have the most extensive access to Putah Creek away from I-80. If you start at Old Davis Road, access from I-80 is the easiest, and you can still take advantage of a significant portion of the reserve that's some distance from the freeway.

HOPKINS ROAD

The main parking area provides access to numerous picnic tables with fire rings, which makes this a popular place on nice weekends. The trail and Levee Road run west from the parking area for a mile through the quietest portion of the reserve past valley oaks and cottonwood trees to the western terminus at Pedrick Road, where there is a parking lot and restroom. Heading east, it's about 1.7 miles to the Old Davis Road trailhead, the eastern terminus, with a lot of freeway noise as you reach I-80 and then continue beyond it.

OLD DAVIS ROAD

This is your best bet if you want quick access from I-80 and a shorter hike. The trail runs west through open grasslands and oak woodlands, with good access to Putah Creek and the opportunity to observe woodpeckers, mallard ducks, Canada geese, and great blue herons. Beyond the railroad tracks (listen and look both ways before crossing), the freeway noise grows louder as you approach I-80.

33 Putah Creek Nature Park

DISTANCE:	2.0 miles roundtrip
ELEVATION GAIN:	20 feet
HIGH POINT:	135 feet
DIFFICULTY:	Easy
FITNESS:	Walkers, runners
FAMILY-FRIENDLY:	Yes
DOG-FRIENDLY:	On-leash
BIKE-FRIENDLY:	Yes
AMENITIES:	Bathrooms, picnic tables
CONTACT/MAP:	Winters Parks and Recreation; no map online
GPS:	N 38°31.283', W 121°58.079'
MORE KEY INFO:	Open 6 AM to 10 PM

GETTING THERE

Driving: Driving north on Highway 113 in Davis, take the Russell Boulevard exit (exit 28). Go left (west) over Highway 113, then at 0.4 mile bear left to continue on Russell Boulevard. At 7.9 miles, at a meeting with County Road 93A, continue left on Russell Boulevard, and then cross over US Highway 505 (exit 11) and reach the town of Winters at 10.8 miles. West of US 505, the road becomes Grant Avenue (Highway 128); drive 0.9 mile and then turn left on Railroad Avenue. After four short blocks, turn left on East Main Street, go one

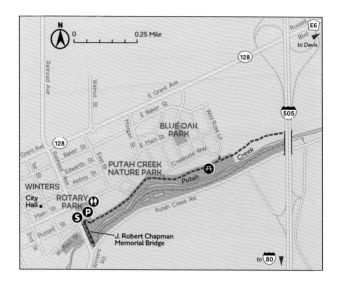

block, and then turn right into the spacious parking lot for Rotary Park.

   Transit: Yolobus route 220 stops at Winters City Hall, two blocks from the trailhead.

Take an easy walk on a paved path along the banks of beautiful Putah Creek. Enjoy the moving water and the lush vegetation along the creek, and then reward yourself by having lunch or dinner at one of the inviting restaurants in Winters.

GET MOVING

Start your stroll by heading back to Railroad Avenue from the parking lot and walk south one block to the J. Robert Chapman Memorial Bridge. The bridge is named for a former member of the Winters City Council who was instrumental in the 2006 renovation of the historic structure. Built in 1906 for the Vaca Valley Railroad to help ship local goods south to Vacaville, the bridge is a major source of pride in Winters, a small agricultural town near US 505 with a relaxed, easygoing charm. Residents and visitors alike, whether walking, running, or biking, use the bridge to take advantage of the bird's-eye view of Putah Creek; you'll definitely want to do the same.

While on the bridge and perched above the creek, first look west and upstream at the nearby Coast Range hills. Putah Creek originates to the northwest on the slopes of Cobb Mountain in the Mayacamas Mountains of Lake County. It then flows south and east to Winters, getting dammed twice in the process, first at Lake Berryessa at Monticello Dam and

The sturdy J. Robert Chapman Memorial Bridge across Putah Creek

then farther downstream at Lake Solano at the Putah Diversion Dam, which sends a substantial amount of water south to Solano County for irrigation purposes.

Next look east and downstream. You'll see the waters of Putah Creek coursing between cottonwoods and willows on the gentle journey east to Davis through fertile Sacramento Valley farmlands; Putah Creek forms the border between Yolo County and Solano County along the way. In Davis its waters are channeled away from the town and into the artificial South Fork Putah Creek (see Trail 32, Putah Creek Riparian Reserve) before entering the Yolo Bypass and then the Sacramento River Deep Water Ship Channel.

When you're ready to start the actual walk, go back to the north side of the bridge and take the broad paved path on the right that goes east, or downstream. After 150 feet a dirt path descends to the creek; several more such paths depart along the length of the route, all worth exploring. Houses range along the left (north) side of the trail and you'll also go by a community garden. The route soon passes the first of several trailside benches.

However, it's Putah Creek and its floodplain and banks that will draw your attention. Stately cottonwoods tower over supple willows along the stream and on the floodplain. Valley oaks provide ample shade in the deep and rich soil farther up the slopes and along the flats above the creek, joined by numerous nonnative eucalyptus trees. In spring look for lupines, California poppies, and other wildflowers. Canada geese, mallards, and other water-loving birds fly near the water, while woodpeckers, scrub jays, mourning doves, crows, and a wide variety of songbirds spend their time near the banks and in the oak woodlands.

The path gently descends to its lowest point at 0.2 mile from the trailhead, its closest approach to Putah Creek. From here the path rises ever so gently into uplands shaded by valley oaks. Access paths lead in from the neighborhood on the left. Pass a picnic table and then reach the end of the paved trail at 0.6 mile when it curves left to end at Creekside Way.

This is a good spot to turn around and head back, or you can continue on the dirt path. It passes an open field before the surface turns back to pavement at 0.8 mile. The path itself ends at 1.0 mile at US 505. One bonus for having gone this far: you have excellent westward views of Pleasants Ridge and the Vaca Mountains in the Coast Range as you head back.

GO FARTHER

You can also explore the south bank of Putah Creek. Cross the J. Robert Chapman Memorial Bridge, take the steps on the right (west), and explore the dirt path that runs downstream (east) near the banks of Putah Creek. It runs east for a mile to pass under US 505. Also consider exploring downtown Winters and the surrounding neighborhoods.

34   Blue Ridge Trail

DISTANCE:	5.4 miles roundtrip
ELEVATION GAIN:	1700 feet
HIGH POINT:	1585 feet
DIFFICULTY:	Challenging
FITNESS:	Hikers
FAMILY-FRIENDLY:	No
DOG-FRIENDLY:	No
BIKE-FRIENDLY:	No
AMENITIES:	Restroom at lower parking lot
CONTACT/MAP:	UC Davis Natural Reserves; map on website
GPS:	N 38°30.704', W 122°5.814'
MORE KEY INFO:	Hiking prohibited on Cal Fire red flag days; potentially dangerous creek crossing; steep trail with no shade; bring plenty of water; poison oak; area burned in 2020; check with UC Davis for current conditions

GETTING THERE

Driving: Driving north on Highway 113 in Davis, take the Russell Boulevard exit (exit 28). Go left (west) over Highway 113, then at 0.4 mile bear left to continue on Russell Boulevard. At 7.9 miles, at a meeting with County Road 93A, continue left on Russell Boulevard, and then cross over US Highway 505 and reach the town of Winters at 10.8 miles. West of US 505, the road becomes Grant Avenue (Highway 128). Drive through and beyond Winters on Highway 128, and at 9.7 miles, cross Putah Creek on a bridge. Immediately after crossing the creek, turn right into the main trailhead parking lot. Additional parking is available another 0.2 mile up Highway 128 on the right, just across from the trailhead.

This challenging hike is most suitable for the physically fit and reasonably agile. You'll climb 1700 feet in elevation, at times on rocky and slippery tread, but you'll be rewarded with a 360-degree view over Lake Berryessa and the Coast Range mountains stretching as far as the eye can see. You'll also see evidence of the 2015 Wragg Fire, but much of the vegetation has already recovered. As noted above, entrance is prohibited on Cal Fire red flag days, and the crossing of Cold Canyon Creek can be dangerous after major rainstorms.

GET MOVING

If you parked at the lower lot, find the dirt road near Cold Canyon Creek and go left (south) for 200 yards. If there is no water in Cold Canyon Creek, walk through the culvert under Highway 128 and follow a path on the other side that quickly joins the main trail on the far (south) side of Highway 128; if there's water in the culvert, take the dirt path on the left (east) side of Cold Canyon Creek that climbs to the parking lot on Highway 128. Carefully cross Highway 128 to a gate and then continue on the main path away from the road.

Go 0.1 mile to a trail fork. The Homestead Trail (Trail 35) runs to the left on the east side of the creek. You go right and immediately cross Cold Canyon Creek—no problem when there's little or no water flow, but after major rains in winter and spring you may have to wade. If the flow is too strong, choose caution and hike another day when the water flow is lower.

Once across the stream, start a long upward climb made easier by the sinuous switchbacks that moderate the steepness. The blackened remains of oak trees provide ample evidence of the 2015 Wragg Fire that roared through the area; higher up on Blue Ridge you'll see some modest evidence of burnt vegetation, but there the chaparral has recovered quickly—as it has evolved to do after a wildfire.

The first views of Blue Ridge come soon into view. You'll certainly notice multiple vultures circling lazily around the heights, hoping hikers like you will drop dead so they can have a feast. Use that thought to make sure you have followed all the precautions for this hike: bring more than plenty of water for everyone in your group and hike on a day with moderate temperatures and no Cal Fire red flag warning.

Looking out at Lake Berryessa from the Blue Ridge Trail

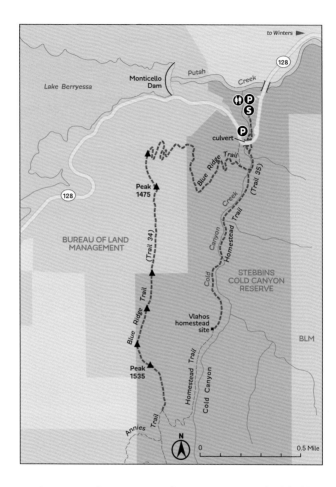

As you continue up, pause in an open area to look behind to the east. Cold Canyon lies below, holding the Homestead Trail and a mix of green vegetation interspersed with modest evidence of the Wragg Fire. Just to the east looms Pleasants Ridge, while Putah Creek courses through the valley to the north.

The switchbacks continue up through chaparral until you finally reach the ridge at 1.6 miles from the trailhead. The path narrows, turns south, then reaches the first of five small peaks.

Stop to catch your breath here and take in the full panorama you've worked so hard to win. Just below to the west the broad expanse of Lake Berryessa probes the low spots in the Mayacamas Mountains, part of the much larger Coast Range that extends along much of California and farther north into the Pacific Northwest. Look north by northwest toward Clear Lake to spy Cobb Mountain on the horizon, the highest peak in the Mayacamas at 4724 feet. Views are spectacular in all directions; if it's an especially clear day, you can look east through the gap created by Putah Creek at the Sacramento Valley and far beyond to the Sierra Nevada, snow-capped from winter well into summer.

From here on, the Blue Ridge Trail is narrow and rocky as well as slippery on the steeper sections. Always watch your step and make sure to stay on the main path that runs on or very near the spine of the ridge. As you walk, notice the rock itself, both at your feet and around you in exposed areas. It's composed primarily of sedimentary layers deposited many millions of years ago on the floor of the Pacific Ocean, later raised and folded onto the North American continent by the collision of the Pacific and North American tectonic plates.

The Blue Ridge Trail passes through thick chaparral, with large amounts of chamise. The views will always be with you, with a changing perspective on Lake Berryessa and the surrounding mountains that will keep you reaching for your camera. The fourth peak, the highest of the five, is yours at 2.4 miles, elevation 1585 feet. Continue on to the fifth peak and then drop down to the official end of this hike at 2.7 miles at the junction with Annies Trail and the trail that drops east down to Cold Canyon and the Homestead Trail. You can retrace your steps and return along this trail to the trailhead for a 5.4-mile round-trip or continue as described in Go Farther.

GO FARTHER

If you go left at the end, you can make a 4.9-mile loop with the Homestead Trail (Trail 35). The path plunges steeply east, losing 400 feet over a half mile. Then it swings north and descends through Cold Canyon 0.5 mile to the Vlahos homestead site. From here, the trailhead is downhill another 1.2 miles north. Pop out onto Highway 128 and head back to your vehicle. Wear sturdy shoes if you try this loop.

35 Homestead Trail

DISTANCE:	2.4 miles roundtrip
ELEVATION GAIN:	450 feet
HIGH POINT:	725 feet
DIFFICULTY:	Moderate
FITNESS:	Hikers
FAMILY-FRIENDLY:	Yes, but creek crossing can be dangerous; a lot of trailside poison oak
DOG-FRIENDLY:	No
BIKE-FRIENDLY:	No
AMENITIES:	Restroom at lower parking lot
CONTACT/MAP:	UC Davis Natural Reserves; map on website
GPS:	N 38˚30.704', W 122˚5.814'
MORE KEY INFO:	Hiking prohibited on Cal Fire red flag days; potentially dangerous creek crossing; a lot of trailside poison oak; area burned in 2020; check with UC Davis for current conditions

GETTING THERE

Driving: Driving north on Highway 113 in Davis, take the Russell Boulevard exit (exit 28). Go left (west) over Highway 113, then at 0.4 mile bear left to continue on Russell Boulevard. At 7.9 miles, at a meeting with County Road 93A, continue left on Russell Boulevard, and then cross over US Highway 505 and reach the town of Winters at 10.8 miles. West of US 505, the road becomes Grant Avenue (Highway 128). Drive

The sloping ridge on the east side of Cold Canyon Creek

through and beyond Winters on Highway 128, and at 9.7 miles, cross Putah Creek on a bridge. Immediately after crossing the creek, turn right into the main trailhead parking lot. Additional parking is available another 0.2 mile up Highway 128 on the right, just across from the trailhead.

Wander upstream along Cold Canyon Creek in the UC Davis Stebbins Cold Canyon Reserve. This popular trail passes an impressive variety of foothill plant species to end at the remnants of the Vlahos homestead site. Much of this area burned in the 2015 Wragg Fire; you'll definitely see evidence of the conflagration, but the vegetation has recovered well, and most trees along the path were spared. As noted above, entrance is prohibited on Cal Fire red flag days, and the crossing of Cold Canyon Creek can be dangerous after major rainstorms.

GET MOVING

If you parked at the lower lot, find the dirt road near Cold Canyon Creek and go left (south) for 200 yards. If there is no water in Cold Canyon Creek, walk through the culvert under Highway 128 and follow a path on the other side that quickly joins the main trail on the far (south) side of Highway 128 before reaching the official trailhead; if there's water in the culvert, take the dirt path on the left (east) side of Cold Canyon Creek that climbs to the parking lot on Highway 128. Carefully cross Highway 128 to a gate and then continue on the main path away from the road.

At 0.1 mile the Blue Ridge Trail (Trail 34) goes right to cross the creek. Stay left to reach the official beginning of the Homestead Trail where you sign the register for Stebbins Cold Canyon Reserve. Be sure to read all the warning signs, which include heatstroke dangers when combining this hike with the Blue Ridge Trail (see Go Farther).

Continue the upstream journey on the Homestead Trail. Plant life is especially diverse in Cold Canyon. Tree species include gray pine, blue oak, and interior live oak on the drier areas and on the slopes, with California laurel (bay), cottonwood, and big-leaf maple in the moister areas near the creek. There's also plenty of trailside buckeye, which has large compound leaves and sports spikes of showy flowers in late spring. Understory chaparral plants include redbud, scrub oak, toyon, manzanita, coyote brush, yerba santa, and chamise. Visit from March to May for wildflowers, including shooting stars, *Brodiaea*, red and blue larkspur, and more.

Occasional gaps in vegetation allow you to look westward up the steep slope to the rocky spine of Blue Ridge. The only crossing of Cold Canyon Creek on this trail is at 0.7 mile. The creek is dry or nearly so in summer until substantial rains come in fall. In winter and spring, flow can be strong, especially after major rainstorms. You may be able to rock-hop or you might have to wade; if the flow is too strong, turn around and return to the trailhead.

The trail continues gently south and upward on the west side of the creek to a trail fork at 1.2 miles. Go left to reach the remains of the Vlahos homestead site, the terminus of this hike. Several decades ago, goats grazed here, and John Vlahos produced milk and cheese. You can still visit the cold storage area, but most other evidence of the home and dairy has vanished. After you're done imagining yourself back in the Vlahos dairy days, turn around and return the way you came for a 2.4-mile round-trip or continue as described in Go Farther.

GO FARTHER

You can do a 4.9-mile loop with the Blue Ridge Trail (Trail 34). From the trail fork at 1.2 miles beside the Vlahos homesite site, go right to ascend gently for 0.5 mile and then climb 0.5 mile up the ridge (aided by numerous wooden steps) to the terminus of Trail 34, where the Blue Ridge Trail and Annies Trail meet, allowing you to make a full loop. Be forewarned that this last half-mile section is very steep (400 feet of elevation gain) and slippery. Make sure you and your party are physically prepared and have proper footwear—and that you have plenty of water, especially on warm days.

ACKNOWLEDGMENTS

My deepest thanks to the many people who gave me advice, shared key information, and read portions of this manuscript for accuracy: Kent Anderson, Putah Creek Council; Emily Bertram, Marshall Gold Discovery State Historic Park; Terry Cook, California State Capitol Museum; Andrew Fulks, UC Davis Arboretum; Joe Hobbs, Yolo Bypass Wildlife Area; Jeff Horn, Bureau of Land Management, Mother Lode Field Office; Harry McQuillen, Cosumnes River Preserve; Eric Peach, Protect American River Canyons; Rich Preston, Folsom Lake State Recreation Area; Lauren Shoemaker, Auburn State Recreation Area; Eric Thomsen, California State Capitol Museum; Beatrix Treiterer, Stone Lakes National Wildlife Refuge; Nancy Ullrey, Cache Creek Nature Preserve; and Dan White, Lodi Parks and Recreation.

RESOURCES

TRAIL AND PARK MANAGEMENT AGENCIES

Auburn State Recreation Area
530-885-4527
www.parks.ca.gov/?page_id=502

Bureau of Land Management, Mother Lode Field Office
916-941-3101
www.blm.gov/office
/mother-lode-field-office

Cache Creek Nature Preserve
530-661-1070
https://cachecreekconservancy
.org

California State Capitol Museum
916-324-0333
www.parks.ca.gov/?page_id=495
http://capitolmuseum.ca.gov

Cosumnes River Preserve
916-684-2816
www.cosumnes.org

Davis Parks and Community Services
530-757-5626
https://cityofdavis.org/city-hall
/parks-and-community-services

Effie Yeaw Nature Center
916-489-4918
www.sacnaturecenter.net

Folsom Lake State Recreation Area
916-988-0205
www.parks.ca.gov/?page_id=500

Lodi Parks and Recreation
209-333-6742
www.lodi.gov/258
/Parks-Recreation

Marshall Gold Discovery State Historic Park
530-622-3470
www.parks.ca.gov/?page_id=484

Old Sacramento State Historic Park
916-445-7387
www.parks.ca.gov/?page_id=497

Placer County Parks and Trails
530-886-4901
www.placer.ca.gov/Parks

**Sacramento City Parks
and Recreation**
916-808-5200
www.cityofsacramento.org
/ParksandRec/Parks

**Sacramento County
Regional Parks**
916-875-6961
www.regionalparks.saccounty
.net/Pages/default.aspx

**Sacramento Municipal
Utilities District**
888-742-7683
www.smud.org

**Stone Lakes National
Wildlife Refuge**
916-775-4421
www.fws.gov/refuge/Stone_Lakes

UC Davis Arboretum
530-752-4880
https://arboretum.ucdavis.edu

UC Davis Natural Reserves
https://naturalreserves
.ucdavis.edu

Winters Parks and Recreation
530-794-6700
www.cityofwinters.org
/parks-and-recreation

Yolo Bypass Wildlife Area
530-757-2461
www.wildlife.ca.gov/Lands/Places
-to-Visit/Yolo-Bypass-WA

TRAIL AND CONSERVATION ORGANIZATIONS

American River Conservancy
www.arconservancy.org

**American River
Parkway Foundation**
https://arpf.org

Cache Creek Conservancy
https://cachecreekconservancy
.org

Canyon Keepers
www.canyonkeepers.org

Effie Yeaw Nature Center
www.sacnaturecenter.net

**Friends of Lakes Folsom
and Natoma**
http://folfan.org

**Friends of Stone Lakes
National Wildlife Refuge**
www.friendsofstonelakes.org

**Friends of the UC
Davis Arboretum**
https://arboretum.ucdavis.edu
/support

**Gold Discovery
Park Association**
www.marshallgold.com

**Leave No Trace Center
for Outdoor Ethics**
https://lnt.org

Mother Lode Trails
www.motherlodetrails.org

**Protect American
River Canyons**
www.parc-auburn.org

Putah Creek Council
www.putahcreekcouncil.org

Sacramento Audubon Society
www.sacramentoaudubon.org

**Sacramento Valley
Conservancy**
www.sacramentovalley
conservancy.org

**Save the American
River Association**
www.sarariverwatch.org

**Sierra Club Mother
Lode Chapter**
www.sierraclub.org/mother-lode

Tuleyome
http://tuleyome.org

Yolo Basin Foundation
http://yolobasin.org

INDEX

ABOUT THE AUTHOR

Northern California native **John Soares** grew up near Redding hiking in the foothills near Anderson. He has lived in Crescent City, Klamath, Chico, Davis, and Mount Shasta. John has hiked all over the American West, as well as Canada, Europe, and Central America. He is the author of *Day Hiking: Mount Shasta, Lassen & Trinity Alps Regions*; *100 Classic Hikes: Northern California* (now in a fourth edition); and *Hike the Parks: Redwood National and State Parks*.

Stephanie Hoffman

As a freelance writer, John works with businesses and nonprofit organizations (JohnWrites.net) and writes for magazines and newspapers. He lives in Ashland, Oregon. For hiking tips, visit NorthernCaliforniaHikingTrails.com.

MOUNTAINEERS BOOKS

SKIPSTONE · BRAIDED RIVER

recreation · lifestyle · conservation

MOUNTAINEERS BOOKS, including its two imprints, Skipstone and Braided River, is a leading publisher of quality outdoor recreation, sustainability, and conservation titles. As a 501(c)(3) nonprofit, we are committed to supporting the environmental and educational goals of our organization by providing expert information on human-powered adventure, sustainable practices at home and on the trail, and preservation of wilderness.

Our publications are made possible through the generosity of donors, and through sales of 700 titles on outdoor recreation, sustainable lifestyle, and conservation. To donate, purchase books, or learn more, visit us online:

MOUNTAINEERS BOOKS
1001 SW Klickitat Way, Suite 201 • Seattle, WA 98134
800-553-4453 • mbooks@mountaineersbooks.org
www.mountaineersbooks.org

An independent nonprofit publisher since 1960

YOU MAY ALSO LIKE:

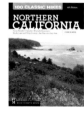